"So many things clamor for our attention during this season when we really do want to put our focus on Christ. Sinclair Ferguson helps us to turn our gaze toward Jesus day by day so that we can take in the wonder of his grace toward sinners."

NANCY GUTHRIE, Bible teacher and Author

"If, like me, you have been guilty of largely ignoring the 40 days of Lent, prepare to be redirected, challenged and stirred by Sinclair Ferguson's focus, not on the process but on the person and work of the Lord Jesus."

ALISTAIR BEGG, Senior Pastor, Parkside Church, Cleveland; Bible teacher, Truth for Life

"I've peppered Sinclair with questions over a lunch table. I've read his books. I listen to his sermons. All because he is a precious guide to understanding our Savior's life and work. And that's the glorious effect of reading this devotional. Read it during Lent. Read it before Lent. Read it after Lent. It doesn't matter. Just be sure to read it."

TONY REINKE, Author

"Sinclair Ferguson's Lent book is both wonderfully accessible and theologically rich. The daily comments are not too long to intimidate nor too short to be unsatisfying. Both younger and older believers will find much to encourage, challenge and stimulate them in their faith in our Lord Jesus. Some of the insights moved me to tears in deepening my own appreciation of Christ. What a precious resource for God's people."

ANGUS MACLEAY, Rector, St Nicholas Church, Sevenoaks, UK

"We enter holy ground when we follow our Lord's road to the cross. There could be no more reliable guide than Sinclair Ferguson. These readings provide warm encouragement and also a challenge to ongoing, daily repentance—helpful for any time of the year."

DR SHARON JAMES, Social Policy Analyst,
The Christian Institute

"These superb reflections on the journey of Jesus to the cross, as recorded by Luke, are the ideal preparation for Easter. Warm, clear and illuminating, they show us ourselves as we see how Jesus dealt with people on the way. But most of all they show us Jesus, the wonder of his love and his call to follow him as his disciples. Read, enjoy and benefit."

RT REV. WALLACE BENN, Former Bishop of Lewes

"These Lent devotions describe familiar encounters with Jesus in a fresh and challenging way. The reader is encouraged throughout to ask themselves, 'How will I respond to Jesus' words?' Each day's read is short enough to be manageable but deep enough to get to the heart of who Jesus is and what it means to follow him."

CELIA REYNOLDS, Women's Ministry Co-ordinator,
Christchurch Market Harborough

SINCLAIR B. FERGUSON

—

TO SEEK
AND
TO SAVE

—

DAILY REFLECTIONS ON THE
ROAD TO THE CROSS

thegoodbook
COMPANY

To Seek and to Save
© Sinclair B. Ferguson 2020.

Published by:
The Good Book Company

thegoodbook.com | thegoodbook.co.uk
thegoodbook.com.au | thegoodbook.co.nz | thegoodbook.co.in

A CIP catalogue record for this book is available from the British Library.

ISBN: 9781784984458 | Printed in Denmark

Design by André Parker

CONTENTS

INTRODUCTION

Wweread a lot of poetry at school, but among my favourites were the vivid narratives in Geoffrey Chaucer's *The Canterbury Tales*.

There was something fascinating about the characters en route to Canterbury that Chaucer portrayed—pilgrims on their way to visit the shrine of Archbishop Thomas Becket. These included such memorable individuals as the much-married Wife of Bath and the "verray, parfit gentil" Knight. But—no doubt somewhat prejudiced by a sense that I was being called to be a minister—my favourite pilgrim was the poor Parson, who preached the message of Christ but first followed it himself.

But Chaucer was by no means the first author to use a journey as the motif for introducing his readers to a variety of interesting people. He had long been preceded by Luke, the beloved physician and author of the New Testament's third Gospel. From chapter 9 verse 51 onwards, Luke records all the events in Jesus' life in the form of a journey to Jerusalem. This travelogue eventually brings us to Calvary and to the empty tomb.

The narrative begins against the background of a major turning point in the ministry of Jesus. Simon Peter has just confessed that Jesus is the Messiah (9:18-20). In response

Jesus explains that he is going to suffer and be rejected and yet rise again (9:21-22).[1] A week later he is gloriously transfigured in the presence of three of his disciples: Peter, James and John (9:28-36). Again, he tells them about his impending suffering (9:43-45). From virtually that point on, until he enters Jerusalem with the shouts of the people ringing in his ears, everything we learn about Jesus takes place on a journey whose destination is Calvary.

In his travelogue, Luke describes Jesus' encounters with a wide variety of individuals and groups of people. Each of them is described within the scope of only a few verses; but all of them come alive to us through Luke's pen.

In this series of reflections for Lent, we will listen in on most of these conversations.

Each encounter will build up a picture of the journey's real purpose; for, as he tells one man he meets along the way, Jesus is "the Son of Man [who] came to seek and to save the lost" (19:10). We will see Jesus "seeking" out people as he reveals their hearts, perceives their needs and tests their motives. We will see him throwing wide the offer of salvation to those he meets—Jew and Gentile, rich and poor, men and women, all similarly lost. And finally, at the journey's end, we will see him secure that salvation once and for all, at the cost of his life.

But Jesus also issues a challenge to anyone who would follow him along the road to Jerusalem. At the great turning point he says:

> *If anyone would come after me, let him deny himself and take up his cross daily and follow me. For*

---

1 *Note:* References in Luke's Gospel give chapter and verse only, but full references are given for other books of the Bible. All emphases are the author's own.

whoever would save his life will lose it, but whoever loses his life for my sake will save it. For what does it profit a man if he gains the whole world and loses or forfeits himself? (9:23-25)

The key issues for all of those who encounter Jesus in Luke's Gospel are these: Do they know why he is on the road in the first place? And, will they follow him as his disciple?

This Lent, Jesus asks those same questions of us.

ASH WEDNESDAY

THE DISCIPLES WHO NOTICED THE MARK

Luke 9:51

I must have "seen" Ash Wednesday before having any idea of what it was. In my childhood, sometime in February or occasionally in March, I would notice someone with a dirty mark on their forehead—and then another person, and then another. It must have meant something, surely? (We were Scottish Presbyterians. Lent was not something we observed!)

Ash Wednesday was originally the day in the church year when people who were ordered to show public peni tence for their sins began forty days of penance—outward displays of inward repentance. Sometime around the end of the first millennium the practice became more general. The symbol of this was marking the forehead with ashes. It was the sign that a person had begun a multi-week fast, with forty weekdays included. They were now setting out on an internal journey of the spirit that would end only with the celebration of Christ's resurrection at Easter. The message was visible on their faces.

Luke tells us that shortly after Jesus had told his disciples about his forthcoming suffering, they began to notice a mark on his face too. It was not a physical *mark*, but a different *look*—as though something within was manifesting itself in his demeanour:

When the days drew near for him to be taken up, he
set his face to go to Jerusalem. (9:51)

Jerusalem had always been in his sights. At the beginning of his ministry he had been baptised with water from the River Jordan, which was already symbolically saturated with the sins of the people (3:1-22). But now he was heading towards the real baptism which his water baptism had signified: "I have a baptism to be baptised with, and how great is my distress until it is accomplished" (12:50). Now the mark of death was beginning to become visible on his forehead. Now, for Jesus, the prolonged "Lent" that would lead to Calvary and Easter had begun.

On the road to Jerusalem, Jesus encountered a wide variety of people. There was something they all had in common: they were either drawn to him in their need or repelled from him by their pride. No one was neutral. The first of them were those disciples who had been told, but had not immediately taken in, the meaning of the look on his face (9:21-27). It was the outward expression of his inner "distress". The question was, would it repel them or would they follow him?

But perhaps, before we travel any further along this road, we need a word of caution. The people we will meet, not least the disciples, are indeed endlessly interesting. But they are not the focus of the story. In watching them, we must never lose sight of Jesus; for if we do, all we are doing is meeting some fascinating people, and even seeing ourselves reflected in them (good things in themselves). But if that is all we see, we have missed the point. The real point is to see who Jesus is.

So, just as Jesus kept his sights fixed on his destination all the way along the road to Jerusalem, make sure you keep your eyes on him; for this is the key not only to this journey but to understanding the whole gospel message.

REFLECT

- When you read the Gospels, do you tend to look for Jesus or only for a reflection of yourself? What do you see of Jesus in this verse that moves you to praise him?

RESPOND

THURSDAY

THE SONS OF THUNDER

Luke 9:51-55

We were sitting this morning in a coffee shop when some teachers with a whole group of pupils in tow arrived unannounced. The look of mild horror on the face of the one barista on duty was quite a picture! A warning phone call would have helped prepare the way! It would have been a courtesy.

Jesus promoted a courtesy culture. His lifestyle was full of grace. That partly explains why he sent ahead some of the disciples to a Samaritan village with an advance request to receive him and his friends. There were at least thirteen of them; but Luke has already given his readers hints that a larger group usually travelled with him (e.g. in 8:1-3).

When the advance party made their request, the answer was a decided "Not welcome here!"

The problem was not simply a matter of numbers. It was proverbial in Jesus' day that "Jews have no dealings with Samaritans" (John 4:9). Were the Samaritans just similarly racist towards Jesus? It looks as though one of the apostles had let slip, *We are on our way to Jerusalem*. Did one of the villagers spit out the words another Samaritan had used:

"Our fathers worshipped on this mountain, but you [Jews] say that in Jerusalem is the place where people ought to worship" (John 4:20)? *On your way! Not welcome here!*

Luke passes over the Samaritan villagers' response. His camera is focused on the encounter between the brothers James and John and the Lord Jesus. The two brothers were indignant. They responded, "Lord, do you want us to tell fire to come down from heaven and consume them?" (9:54). James and John were not given the nickname "Sons of Thunder" for nothing (Mark 3:17). This outrage was their natural—if massively extreme—reaction.

Who did they think they were—Elijah? (The story is told in 2 Kings 1:1-16.) They couldn't control their fire-filled tempers, let alone direct heavenly fire to a village on earth! And more than that, they obviously had miscalculated, for Jesus "turned and rebuked them" (9:55).

These are interesting words, don't you think?

Luke tells us that Jesus "*turned*". What does that suggest? Had they been talking at Jesus' back as he quietly resumed his journey without fuss? If so, then James and John were not only irritated by the Samaritans; they were rude to Jesus—under the guise of a question, they were telling their Master what they thought he should be doing.

Look at Jesus. Unlike James and John, he accepted rejection as part of God's sovereign providence in his life. He responded with meekness. The sons of thunder wanted to destroy Samaritans; but the Son of Man had come to save Samaritans as well as Jews.

We tend to think of John as the "apostle of love", not as a "son of thunder". But it was only by grace that he learned to love like his Saviour. The John we meet in Luke's Gospel didn't suffer gladly those he regarded as fools and perhaps thought this was a virtue. Some Christians today make the same mistake. But "love ... does not insist on its own way;

it is not irritable" (1 Corinthians 13:4). For Jesus did not insist on his own way (Romans 15:3), either then in Samaria or later in Gethsemane (22:42).

Has it ever dawned on you what Jesus was really like? And has that made you want to be like him?

REFLECT

• Think back to a recent incident when you experienced rejection. If the great test of love is how we handle rejection, what did your response reveal about you? How does John's story give you hope?

RESPOND

FRIDAY

THREE MEN ON THE ROAD

Luke 9:57-62

My father coined an expression that he often used to make it clear to me that I was not thinking clearly: "Your head is full of broken glass!"

This (admittedly unusual) expression makes an important point. Wrong thinking means something is broken inside your mind; and wrong thinking can have painful consequences. Jesus is on his way to Jerusalem, to suffer and die. He encounters three men, apparently in quick succession. In each case he questions whether they are thinking straight about what it means to be his disciple (the dominant term for a Christian in the Gospels and Acts).

The first man offers to follow Jesus without being invited. His enthusiasm knows no bounds. He confidently asserts that he will follow Jesus wherever he lays his head. *But what if there is no bed?* asks Jesus.

Three young men once arrived at a mission I was leading and announced, "The Lord has told us to join you". I said that since the Lord had not given me advance warning, no sleeping arrangements had been made for them, and so they would have to sleep on the floor. They were nowhere to be found the next morning. It seems they had not reckoned on the fact that those who follow Jesus may have no pillow on which to lay their heads!

Unlike the first man, who volunteers, the second man is called by Jesus to follow him. However, he wants to wait until after his father's funeral. Was it just about to take place? Judging by Jesus' response, the man's father was still alive. He was saying, *Yes, I will follow you... but later*. The Lord gives a famous, somewhat enigmatic, and possibly proverbial response: "Leave the dead to bury their own dead." In essence, when it comes to following Jesus, nothing else, not even family ties, can be allowed to take priority. Nothing and nobody—period—must take priority over Jesus.

The third man, like the first, also volunteers, but with a little more caution. (Had he overheard the first two conversations?) Wisdom dictates that he state a minor qualification up front. He would like to say his goodbyes at home—a modest request surely. And perhaps a carefully thought-out one, since it echoes Elisha's words when Elijah called him for future service (1 Kings 19:19-21). Jesus responds in kind when he says that no one who puts his hand to the plough and then looks back is fit for the kingdom of God. His reference to a plough reminds this man of what Elisha actually did when he asked, "Let me kiss my father and my mother, and then I will follow you"—exactly that! Elisha immediately kissed his past life goodbye. He took the twelve yoke of oxen with which he had been ploughing (he must have come from a wealthy family), sacrificed them, cooked the meat on a fire kindled by burning the wood of the yokes, and held a becoming-a-trainee-prophet party for his friends. It was the farming equivalent of burning his boats.

Earlier in the Gospel, Luke had recorded Jesus' parable of the Sower (8:4-8). The same seed (God's word) falls on three kinds of soil which bear no lasting fruit. The seed sometimes falls on the hard pathway and is snatched away; it some-times falls on shallow soil with a rocky substratum, where there is immediate joy but no repentance; and sometimes the seed falls on thorny ground, where "the cares and riches and pleasures of life" choke it. These men were simply test cases for that parable. As far as we know, they turned out just as the parable suggested.

Jesus does not call every disciple to leave home. Earlier in this Gospel, he told a man who wanted to follow him to go home and serve him there (8:38-39). But what this passage teaches us is that Jesus wants "I am willing to give up everything, go anywhere, do anything for you" disciples.

REFLECT

- What reservations do you have about Christ's lordship over your life? What gives you confidence that he is worth following?

RESPOND

SATURDAY

THE SELF-DEFENCE LAWYER

Luke 10:25-37

These verses contain one of the most famous parables in the New Testament. Can you picture the scene?

Jesus is busily engaged in his ministry, teaching about the kingdom of God. A distinguished figure stands up. Perhaps his accent or tone of voice gives him away. He is a lawyer and is planning to put Jesus to the test. Perhaps he even wants to put Jesus in his place as an uneducated Galilean with no legal or biblical training! So, he asks a question calculated to trap him but thinly veiled as a genuine theological enquiry: *How do I find eternal life?* It's a great question, isn't it?

Jesus asks the lawyer to tell him what the law says. It reminds us of the adage, "Why does a rabbi always answer a question with a question? Answer: why not?" There's a lot of wisdom in that principle; Christians need to learn it.

Jesus has already put this lawyer on the back foot. He has taken over the questioning! *Love God and love your neighbour* is the reply. *Well,* says Jesus, *live like that!*

The lawyer is probably now wishing he had never asked the question in the first place. He tries to "justify himself" with his own question: "Who is my neighbour?" (v 29). He wanted to test and best Jesus in subtle theological debate; but he now finds that Jesus is testing his lifestyle. So, he answers back, *Just tell me who my neighbours are, then! Give me a list of them!* He is ready to engage in some theological hair-splitting with Jesus.

The lawyer should have known better. For the Saviour went on to tell the story of the Good Man of Samaria who stopped for and cared for the Jew who "fell among robbers" (v 30). But do not gloss over Jesus' punch line in verse 36. He throws the lawyer's question into reverse gear. In essence, he tells the lawyer that he isn't even asking the right question! The real question is, *Who proved to be a neighbour to the man in need?* Answer: the Samaritan.

At this point the smart lawyer must have realised he had dug himself into a hole. He wanted to limit his responsibilities. (*Tell me who my neighbour is, and I'll love him.*) But Jesus tells him there are no lists that he can tick off. Rather, he says, *God calls you to be a loving neighbour to anyone you see in need, irrespective of race or religion, and to go out of your way to help them, even if it is inconvenient and costly.* Silence reigned.

I spoke on this parable one day at a lunchtime gathering in our church. I remember applying it in some such words as: "Given the number of people in this room, it is likely that at least one of us will be tested on this parable before the day is done".

Four hours later, I was walking through the churchyard in the twilight, heading to another meeting. In the gloaming I saw a heap on the ground among the headstones. "Somebody has dumped something" I thought, and like the Levite in Jesus' story I "came to the place and saw...", yes, "*him*". A homeless man was huddled on the ground, cold and hungry. So "one of us" was indeed tested before the day was done. I had not expected to be that one!

Here, in Luke 10, is a man who thought he was testing Jesus. But the reverse was actually true. There was a sting in this tale! It is always that way with Jesus.

REFLECT

- Many people will be reading this page today and reflecting on 10:25-37 at the same time. At least one of us will be tested, surely. How will you respond if it is you? Pray that you will be ready.

RESPOND

THE FIRST WEEK OF LENT

——

CONVERSATIONS
ON THE WAY

SUNDAY

Not what these hands have done
Can save my guilty soul;
Not what my toiling flesh has borne
Can make my spirit whole.
Not what I feel or do
Can give me peace with God;
Not all my prayers and sighs and tears
Can bear my awful load.

Thy work alone, O Christ,
Can ease this weight of sin;
Thy blood alone, O Lamb of God,
Can give me peace within.
Thy love to me, O God,
Not mine, O Lord, to thee,
Can rid me of this dark unrest
And set my spirit free.

Thy grace alone, O God,
To me can pardon speak;
Thy power alone, O Son of God,
Can this sore bondage break.
No other work, save thine,
No other blood will do;
No strength, save that which is divine,
Can bear me safely through.

(Horatius Bonar, 1808-1889)

MONDAY

THE VERY DIFFERENT SISTERS

Luke 10:38-42

Sometimes children seem to weave their personalities and interests into the spaces left by their siblings. One sister plays sports, while the other likes music; one brother likes mathematics, while the other prefers to read, and so on.

It isn't always like that, of course. But it seems that is how it was in one particular household in the village of Bethany—the home of two sisters, Mary and Martha, and their brother Lazarus. Jesus loved their family and was clearly loved by them. The fact that the sisters were very different could not have escaped his notice. Luke gives us a hint. For some reason (perhaps the wording of John 11:1) I always say "Mary and Martha"—in that order. But Luke hints that when Jesus arrived on this occasion, he entered *Martha's* domain. It was she who "welcomed him into *her* house" (10:38)—she ran domestic affairs!

It is a familiar situation. When you enter a house, you can usually tell who runs the home and makes family life work. And you have almost certainly met Martha under some other name. There she is, straining to get everything done.

But sometimes she puts so much pressure on herself to *get things right* that she's on the verge of breaking.

On this occasion, Martha broke big time. Can you see her here? She stands right in front of Jesus ("she went up to him", v 40). She towers over her sister, who is seated at his feet listening to him. There she is, body rigid, arms like pokers at her side, fists tightly clenched, voice higher-pitched than usual. Then comes the explosion. It is a double complaint: one about Jesus ("Lord, do *you* not care?") and the other about Mary ("My *sister* has left me to serve alone"—was she too uptight even to use her name?). And to make matters worse, she tells the Lord exactly what he ought to do about it ("Tell her then to help me")!

It's embarrassing. More than that, it is so unspiritual, isn't it? After all, "Mary has chosen the good portion" (v 42). But Martha is angry with her sister; and she is angry with Jesus too.

The disciples had once reacted in the same way and had even asked the same question ("Do you not care?" Mark 4:38). But they thought they were in danger of drowning! This was only domestic overload. It must have been embarrassing—were the disciples wondering where to look?

Notice how Jesus responds. Like a calm spiritual physician, he traces these symptoms in Martha's reaction back to the root of the problem. But he also responds like a father. There's a lot of emotional concern in the way he repeats her name: "Martha, Martha" (v 41). And there is something inexpressibly gentle about the way he puts his finger on the source of this painful inflammation. He doesn't give her a lecture about losing her temper, or even for that matter about not yielding to God's providence, or about the importance of better organisation and delegating responsibilities.

These may all have their place, but they are not the root of the problem. No, the Lord's diagnosis is simpler: Martha has been "anxious and troubled about many things, but one thing is necessary" (v 41-42).

Did Jesus simply mean that a sandwich would have been fine with him, and then Martha could have sat down beside her sister and talked to him?

That was true. But there's more to it than that. Jesus wants to deal with the way Martha has been *distracted* by "many *things*". The result was that she had lost her focus on Jesus *himself*. These *things* were vehicles for serving him. But in the process of Martha's serving, Jesus himself had been obscured. She had lost sight of the Saviour in the service. Doing things *for him* had taken the place of being *with him*. That, after all, is "the good portion" (v 42). How often we make the same mistake as Martha!

REFLECT

- Is today going to be a busy one? There is so much to do. Indeed, there is so much to do *for* Jesus. Read Paul's words in Philippians 3:13-14, and remember that only "one thing is necessary" (10:42).

RESPOND

Distracted by many things on a Sunday morning. We can lose sight of the saviour ~ in our service. Lost focus on Jesus himself. Doing things for Him can take the place of being with Him. Jesus himself can be obscured.

TUESDAY

THE DISCIPLE WHO WANTED A SIMPLE WAY TO PRAY

Luke 11:1-13

I was seventeen at the time and had just finished my first term at university. I felt I had made some strides in knowing how to pray. Then the Christmas vacation came. I remember attending a Saturday-night service. The minister who led it began to pray—and, listening to him, I realised I had hardly begun to learn to pray; here was someone who spoke to God as though he stood in his presence.

The anonymous disciple in Luke's Gospel must have felt the same way—even more so; for he overheard Jesus pray. No wonder he "said to him, 'Lord, teach us to pray, as John taught his disciples'" (11:1). In response Jesus taught him what has become known universally as "the Lord's Prayer".

In the version Luke records—it seems Jesus taught these words on more than one occasion—there are only thirty-six words in English. It takes less than thirty seconds to say. Yet this is a prayer that lasts a lifetime.

But what exactly was Jesus teaching this man about prayer? Surely not simply to say a thirty-second prayer mantra every so often. For one thing, he expected his disciples to pray together (since we are to say, "Give *us* each day ... forgive *us* ... lead *us* not into temptation").

So what was this anonymous disciple meant to learn—as well as the readers of Luke's Gospel who benefit from this record of that disciple's memory?

One day in 1535, Martin Luther's barber, Peter Beskendorf, told him that he found it difficult to pray and asked for help. Luther responded in a very Luther-like way. He wrote a book—a booklet really, of perhaps seven and a half thousand words—entitled *A Simple Way to Pray*. It has proved so helpful to so many Christians that it remains in print to this day.

Luther suggested that Peter should take each of the phrases in the Lord's Prayer and use them as a framework and stimulus for his own prayers. He taught him to reflect on each statement and develop it in praise and petition.

So, when we call God "Father", we praise him for all he has done in Christ to become our Father, we thank him for his fatherly care, and we remember that he is in heaven where he is worshipped and adored—and so on through each of the petitions.

Luther said that as Peter worked through the Lord's Prayer in this way, he would find himself spending more time praying. Indeed, from having found it difficult to pray, he might come to find it difficult to stop praying—there would be so much to praise and thank God for, and to pray about.

This was Luther's own experience. Indeed, as he grew as a Christian, he often spent hours every day in prayer. He sometimes said he was so busy that he needed to spend more time in prayer!

It is encouraging to think that Dr Luther would write a whole treatise for his barber. It is even more encouraging that the Lord Jesus would take time to help this anonymous disciple who felt he was so far behind his Master in knowing how to pray. As Isaiah said about the Servant of the Lord, "a bruised reed he will not break, and a faintly burning wick he will not quench" (Isaiah 42:3).

If you feel that you know all too little about prayer, remember that Jesus has already given you the first steps and even the first words.

So, "when you pray, say: 'Father, hallowed be your name…'" (11:2).

REFLECT

- While these thoughts are still in your mind, stop and take some time just now to pray through the Lord's Prayer in this way.

RESPOND

WEDNESDAY

THE SPEECHLESS MAN

Luke 11:14-26

My elementary-school teacher sometimes insisted that we sit in complete silence for three minutes. They seemed to last for ever and made us want to speak all the more. But we always knew that at the end of the agonising wait, we would be chatting away as usual.

But imagine being told that you would never be able to speak again. If you still had any voice, you would ask two questions, wouldn't you? "What's wrong, doctor? Is there no cure?"

Jesus could cure those unable to speak and give them a voice. The Gospels record more than one occasion when he did that (Matthew 15:30; Mark 7:37). But in this encounter with Jesus, Luke, "the beloved physician", tells us about a mute man whose inability to speak had a more sinister cause—the presence of a demon.

Luke was not naïve. He does not attribute all physical illness or disability directly to the work of Satan or to demon possession. At times he notes that Jesus simply "healed" people. But here he is very specific—whatever the physical symptoms this man had, the root cause of his disability was not physical. The bondage of his tongue was the result of a deeper bondage.

Jesus cast out the mute demon and the man spoke. Don't you wish you knew what he said? Whatever it was, most people who heard it were awestruck.

Most, but not all. Mixed in with the crowd were two groups of people hostile to Jesus. Some of them accused him of performing the exorcism because he was in league with the devil. Others kept on demanding that if he was really the Messiah, he should prove it by performing some sign from heaven. They had deceived themselves into thinking that if he would do something more spectacular than enabling a mute man to speak, then they would believe.

Were some of the crowd taken in by the self-assurance with which these accusers spoke?

Jesus' response is intriguing. A kingdom or family in which there is internal division cannot survive.

Perhaps these words were intended to operate at two levels.

Level one: Jesus' opponents were a kingdom hopelessly divided. One group was complaining about the sign he had just given them—casting out the demon and restoring the man's speech. The other group kept moving the goalposts: they were asking for a sign when he had just given them one! For all practical purposes, their complaints cancelled out each other.

Level two goes deeper. These men were claiming that Jesus was in league with Satan. But how could that be when he had just cast out one of Satan's minions from this man? Jesus' action was a clear indication of what he had come to do: attack the fully-armed strong man, overcome him, and capture what he possessed.

This is what Jesus is on the road to Jerusalem to accomplish. It has been the plan since the beginning, for he is the long-promised offspring of the woman who was to come to crush the head of the serpent (Genesis 3:15). Already he has defeated the devil in the wilderness; now in Luke's Gospel Jesus is bringing restoration of what is rightfully his; and he is on his way to his decisive victory over Satan on the cross.

We live now in the aftermath of that victory. But we are still waiting for the final destruction of Satan's kingdom. So long as that is so, the evil one will try to get revenge on Jesus by attacking his disciples. The Christian life is a battle right to the end! But in that battle Jesus is the winner. And those who belong to him are on the winning side.

REFLECT

- Do not be puzzled if the Christian life is a battle today. Jesus said it would be. Look out for those moments of conflict, and in the midst of them, rejoice that you are ultimately on the winning side.

RESPOND

THURSDAY

THE HYPER-PIOUS WOMAN

Luke 11:27-28

I worked for fifteen years in Philadelphia, Pennsylvania, and from time to time I enjoyed hearing the famed Philadelphia Orchestra. At the end of virtually every performance, someone in the audience—it always sounded like the same person!—would shout above the applause, "Bravo! Bravo!" or "Brava!"

He could, of course, simply have been an excitable Italian. But I always felt slightly embarrassed by this lone voice. A question always lingered in my mind: is this person simply unable to restrain himself? Or does he feel he possesses a superior capacity to appreciate music that warrants his voice being raised above the clapping? Or is he showing off that, as a musical connoisseur, he knows the right Italian terms to use?

We might wonder similarly about the woman in a crowd who shouted out to Jesus, "Blessed is the womb that bore you, and the breasts at which you nursed" (11:27). What did she think she was doing?

Jesus' response to her is intriguing, isn't it? "Blessed *rather* are those who hear the word of God and keep it!" (v 28). What he is *saying* is clear enough; but what is he *doing*?

On the one hand it looks as though Jesus is being very gentle with her. He does not demean her by dismissing her comments—whether she is praising his mother, Mary, or, for that matter, giving vent to the fact that her own son is a ne'er-do-well so different from Mary's son!

Mary is blessed indeed (Luke has already recorded that Elizabeth had said that, 1:42, 45), but perhaps not for the reason this woman might expect. Jesus indicates that there is more this woman needs to understand—namely, the way in which she can come to be among the blessed: by hearing and keeping the word of God.

This is a word of great wisdom. Perhaps it is especially so if we feel that God has blessed others but not us.

What if, behind this woman's words, there was a life full of hurt because she had never been married, or had lost her husband, or had been unable to have children? Little did she know that the blessing Jesus' mother would experience was a costly one, for Mary had also been told that "a sword will pierce through your own soul" (2:35). In essence, Jesus is saying, *Dear woman, I have indeed had a mother blessed by God, but you too can be blessed. Do not make the mistake of locating true blessing in the providences that surround your life. Rather, hear God's word, trust him and walk in obedience.*

Here is a vital lesson for us: God's providential dealings with us are varied, sometimes painful and often mysterious. But the circumstances he sends us are not the measure of his blessing. His providence is not the rule by which we live. What, then, is?

We *hear* God's word and keep it. The two are connected. Notice the verb—it is *hear*, not *read*. Of course, in Jesus' day people did not have their own Bibles. But even although we do, we should not simply *read* them—we should *hear* them: that is, *listen* and *pay attention* to what our heavenly Father is teaching us. Reading is something we do actively; we are, in some sense, in command. Listening is also an activity—but it is one in which we place our lives under the authority of someone else's voice and obey it. There is a difference.

REFLECT

- How will you ensure that you are not only a reader but a hearer and keeper of God's word? Can you think of times when you have been particularly aware of the blessing that Jesus describes?

RESPOND

FRIDAY

THE OFFENDED PHARISEE

Luke 11:37-54

The first thing my mother said to me when I sat down at the table for dinner was usually "Have you washed your hands?" She knew that most of the time she would have been just as well to say "Go and wash your hands", since I had a track record of indifference to cleanliness! But she tolerated me (as I only now realise fully!). After all, eating with dirty hands is hardly a sin.

Unless, of course, you are a Pharisee. Then it is.

Jesus shocked this particular Pharisee. He had invited Jesus to a meal. The first thing he noticed was that the Lord sat down at the table without bothering to wash his hands.

What offended this man was not that Jesus' hands were physically dirty but that he was ignoring the rituals of the Pharisaic tradition.

Jesus saw his response as a symptom of a serious spiritual sickness.

When I was a young minister, a lady who was responsible for the prize-giving of the church Sunday School asked me where she should put the books the children were later to receive. "Oh, just put them on the communion table,"

I replied casually. She gasped, "On the Holy Table?!" and added that one of her previous ministers "would never have allowed the books to go on the Holy Table". I was young and rather thoughtlessly responded, "It's ok. It's no different from your kitchen table." Perhaps you can imagine the look of horror on her face. I did my best to explain but probably failed to recover the situation!

The table was clearly special for this lady—it was after all the table from which "holy communion" was served. But what makes communion, or the Lord's Supper, "holy" is not the bread, or the wine, or the table—but the Lord himself and the communion we enjoy with him. The table is just a table. But the traditions this woman had been taught had turned it into an object of reverence.

The Pharisees had the same attitude to their traditions and, in this case, to the ritual washing of the hands before eating. But their scrupulous concern about washing hands, and cups and dishes, was not matched by a concern to have clean hearts. They confused the symbol with the reality. And, yes, they made a show of giving alms, but they were not offering their hearts either to man or to God. They tithed every little herb while they were indifferent to justice and love. They loved the prominent seats in the synagogues and to be shown honour in the market. Their religion was essentially self-centred and man-centred. Whatever they seemed to be on the outside—leading figures, devoted men of religion, careful to keep the law— they were in fact inwardly dead. They were more interested in and emotionally committed to their own trivial distinctives than to what really honoured and glorified God: namely, genuine love for him and for their neighbours. They made a pretence of devotion to God in order to be admired by men. Tragically they were spiritually blind but assumed they had 20-20 vision.

Jesus calls them "fools" (11:40). The word means someone who lacks spiritual understanding. It describes the person who, despite appearances, is not living before the face of God. To such a person the superficial becomes important, and the important becomes superficial.

That is something that didn't die out with the Pharisees.

REFLECT

• Jesus described the Pharisees as "hypocrites" (Matthew 23:15-36)—a Greek word for actors who wore masks to play parts in a play. They were one person on the stage but another in real life. But hypocrisy begins to disappear when you realise that your real audience is God. When will you need to remember that today?

RESPOND

SATURDAY

THE GREEDY BROTHER

Luke 12:13-21

"Someone in the crowd said to [Jesus], 'Teacher, tell my brother to divide the inheritance with me'" (v 13). Yet another family squabble about money!

There's a lot about family life in the Bible. Genesis, the very first book, is more or less fifty chapters of stories about family life gone sour. There is also a lot about family life in the Gospels. We get glimpses of Jesus' own family (it was large—the wording of Matthew 13:55-56 suggests he had four brothers and at least three sisters) and also of Peter's family (Jesus healed his mother-in-law). And Jesus told stories about families, like the father who had two sons, one of whom was a prodigal.

Why so much about family? Because, following the creation of man as his image, male and female, family was one of God's next best gifts to mankind. There we belong to each other both biologically and relationally.

So, of course, it was and still is in the cross-hairs of the devil's sights. He knows, as the old adage says, that the worst is always the corruption of the best. So, family life has always been under attack, right from the beginning.

In both obvious and subtle ways, Satan seeks to destroy it.

Most people in the West no longer believe in the devil and so never think this way. But even Christians, who do believe in him, can easily forget about him and fail to detect his mucky paws on their lives. It is hard for us to appreciate that he has been both a liar and a murderer from the beginning (John 8:44).

Against this background it should not surprise us that the voice in the crowd represents a family on the verge of self-destruction, with brother set against brother.

Nor should it surprise us that there seems to be a tone in this man's voice that says, *Jesus, why don't you do something about this?* There's a hint of a common inconsistency here. People who want to have nothing to do with Christ and resent his interference in their lives so long as things are going well then turn around and complain that he does not intervene when things go badly. It is always a danger sign when we start telling the Lord what *he should be doing*.

This man is not asking Jesus to help him cope with his situation or respond well to it. No, he treats Jesus as though he were his servant. He does not realise that he himself needs to be delivered from spiritual bondage.

Spiritual bondage? How do we know that? Because of the parable Jesus then tells the crowd. There he puts his finger on the man's problem.

Mr Rich had a bountiful harvest. He planned to expand his business, to increase his profit margin, and perhaps also to diversify his trade or invest his profits (he was going to store not only "grain" but also "goods", 12:18).

The problem Jesus sees is not expansion or diversification. It goes much deeper than that. It is highlighted by the fact that Mr Rich's soliloquy uses first person singular pronouns eleven times in three lines ("I" six times, "my" five times)! And his plan was hedonistic: "relax, eat, drink, and be merry" (v 19). He doesn't finish his sentence with the words we have come to expect: "for tomorrow you die". But that is what happened. The superglue with which he had secured this world to himself was dissolved. Everything had been his, and now none of it was!

This isn't just a story about the uncertainty of life, although that is a fact. No, Jesus puts his finger on the rich man's real problem. He had made himself his god and treated that god richly; but towards the true God he had been a pauper (v 21). He was a worshipper of the "covetousness ... which is idolatry" (Colossians 3:5). The superglue on his possessions was so strong that he foolishly imagined they were his permanently. But that glue contains a fatal poison which killed him, and he ended up with nothing.

Jesus can be very sobering, can't he? But that is because he wants to save us.

REFLECT

- How strong is the glue between you and your possessions (and how can you tell)? What have you seen of Jesus so far in Luke's Gospel that helps to dissolve its power?

RESPOND

THE SECOND WEEK OF LENT

—

MEETING THE CONFUSED

SUNDAY

I greet thee, who my sure Redeemer art,
My only trust and Saviour of my heart,
Who pain didst undergo for my poor sake;
I pray thee, from our hearts all cares to take.

Thou art the King of mercy and of grace,
Reigning omnipotent in every place:
So come, O King, and our whole being sway;
Shine on us with the light of thy pure day.

Thou art the life, by which alone we live,
And all our substance and our strength receive;
O comfort us in death's approaching hour,
Strong-hearted then to face it by thy power.

Thou hast the true and perfect gentleness,
No harshness hast thou and no bitterness:
Make us to taste the sweet grace found in thee
And ever stay in thy sweet unity.

Our hope is in no other save in thee;
Our faith is built upon thy promise free;
O grant to us such stronger hope and sure
That we can boldly conquer and endure.

(From the Strasbourg Psalter, 1545,
tr. Elizabeth L. Smith, 1817-98)

MONDAY

THE FEARFUL FLOCK

Luke 12:22-34

W e sometimes say it, even although we all know it is very bad psychology. We tell people who are anxious, "Don't worry!" and people who are frightened, "Don't be afraid!" Telling them not to be what they know they are is usually a counsel of despair.

So why did Jesus say both of these things to his disciples (v 22, v 32)? Was he a poor psychologist? Hardly!

We sometimes speak about the "grammar" of the gospel. If you are going to speak any language well, there are grammatical principles you must follow. We usually pick them up intuitively if we are immersed in a language from birth. But when we learn a foreign language, we need to learn how it works. In some cases, the mechanics are very different from those of our mother tongue. If we don't learn the grammar, we will always sound foreign.

If we are going to be Jesus' disciples and follow him, we need to understand how his gospel "works".

He illustrates that principle here. In the grammar of faith, all the *imperatives* in God's word (commands: "this is what you are to do") are rooted in *indicatives* (statements of fact:

"this is what God has done, or will do, for you and in you"). Gospel grammar works like this: it is because of what God has done that, therefore, you are to be this or do that. The grammar of the gospel always has this logic.

Our Lord's teaching session here is an illustration of this gospel grammar.

Notice the emphasised words: "And he said to his disciples, '*Therefore* I tell you, *do not be anxious* about your life ... *For* life is more than food" (v 22-23).

The imperative (command) is, "Do not be anxious". But that would be a counsel of despair to the anxious unless we are given reasons, motives and help that will deliver us from that anxiety.

Jesus does that. Notice the logic of what he is saying:

- *Your life is about much more than what you put into or onto your body.*
- *When you understand what that "much more" is, these other things will no longer dominate your thinking, desiring, or feeling.*
- *The result will be that you will become less and less anxious about other things. What once seemed enormously important will now be seen as of secondary significance.*

Far from being a poor psychologist, the Lord Jesus puts his finger on the very things that advertising executives know make people, young and old, anxious: what we put into our bodies or onto them, and how we look. (Think of all those glossy magazine adverts for a start!)

What relieves Jesus' disciples of this anxiety? Knowing this: if God cares for the birds and for the flowers, *how much more* do you think he cares for you?

Do you see the gospel grammar at work here? He cares for you so much more; *therefore* you can worry so much less!

But how can we be sure that he cares for us? The answer lies in the powerful example of the "how much more" logic of gospel grammar that Paul gives us in Romans 8:32:

- Fact: God "did not spare his own Son but gave him up for us all".
- Implication: If he has done that, "how will he not also with him graciously give us all things?"

Have you begun to learn the grammar that Jesus teaches us?

REFLECT

- *Since God has given his Son to die for me, he will provide me today with everything I really need!* When in your day will you need to remember that?

RESPOND

TUESDAY

THE TELLERS OF TRAGEDY

Luke 13:1-5

How did news travel before there were newspapers, mail, telephones, the internet, or social media? By word of mouth.

So it is here: a group of people turn up who have heard some terrible news. *Jesus, have you heard about the Galileans that Pilate massacred when they were in Jerusalem bringing their sacrifices?*

What did Jesus make of it? How would he explain it?

We know no more about this incident. We do know that there was a sadistic streak in Pontius Pilate. Perhaps those slaughtered were zealots—extremists who engaged in armed resistance against Rome. But Jesus' response to the news indicates that the real question in people's minds was this: if these men were trying to serve God—by resisting Rome in an effort to gain freedom for God's people—why did they die so cruelly? *What had they done to deserve this?*

If we are tempted to dismiss their question, we should pause and reflect on the fact that this is a very common reaction when things go badly wrong: "What have they (or I) done to deserve this?"

This, in part, is the theme of the Old Testament book of Job. Things went badly wrong in Job's life. Three of his friends came to visit him in his profound grief and were willing to sit in silence with him in a poignant week of mourning (Job 2:13). But as soon as they began to speak, they zeroed in on this simple "fact": *Since suffering is the result of sin, you must be suffering because of your sin.*

So how does Jesus handle this age-old issue? In two ways.

First, he teaches that tragedies do not befall people simply because of their own sin. He mentions another tragedy. Part of the Tower of Siloam in Jerusalem had collapsed on a crowd of people, killing eighteen. Had God brought together the worst eighteen sinners in the city to teach the people that if they committed the same sins, they would suffer the same fate? Had these people been "worse offenders than all the others in Jerusalem"? Jesus' answer is *No!* (13:3).

Second, he tells them twice, "Unless you repent, you will all likewise perish" (13:3, 5).

We need to pay close attention to what Jesus is saying. He is not denying that human sin can lead to human tragedy. Actions have consequences. But he is saying categorically that we cannot simply draw straight lines back from human tragedy to personal sin. We do not have the calculus that enables us always to apportion blame in that way. Who can make all the right connections between actions and consequences? Who can separate out the consequences of the fall—and the effect of millennia of human sin—from our own individual sin? Only God himself has the knowledge, wisdom and justice to do that.

What then? Jesus presses home the single most important issue: making sure that we repent of our own sin and turn to God in faith; for there is a court in which our personal sin, and our responsibility for the consequences of our individual actions, will be perfectly assessed.

We therefore need to avoid the folly of trying to work out the incomprehensible ("Why did that happen to them?") while failing to recognise what our own sin deserves at the hands of the God of love we have despised, and the God of holiness we daily offend.

REFLECT

- Thank God that through faith in Jesus Christ there is the forgiveness of sins. But remember that the faith that turns to Christ always involves the repentance that turns away from sin. What do you need to repent of today?

RESPOND

WEDNESDAY

THE BENT-OVER WOMAN

Luke 13:10-17

You could always tell where Jesus would be when the weekly Sabbath came around: in the local synagogue.

Sometimes Christians seem to take a rather gloomy view of the idea of a "day of rest" and find it either oppressive or irrelevant. Paradoxically, some polls suggest that Sunday (the "Sabbath" as it would be now for most Christians) has become the most stressful day of the week for many people!

Jesus would not have been one of them. His soul was soaked in Psalm 92 ("A song for the Sabbath") and in Isaiah 58:13-14 ("call the Sabbath a delight"). He knew it was one of God's creation gifts (Genesis 2:1-3), which was restored in the exodus (Exodus 20:8-11; Deuteronomy 5:12-15). But whereas the Pharisees were neurotic about what could and could not be done on the Sabbath, and created their own rules and regulations around it, Jesus simply enjoyed it as a gift from God that helped to regulate all the days of the week.

"The Sabbath was made for man" (Mark 2:27). It was a great time-and-motion principle for the whole week: work hard for God for six days and enjoy resting in God's presence on the seventh. Very clever, really. To enjoy the Sabbath day required discipline in working habits on the other six days! It was a whole-week pattern for blessing. It helped you work, and it gave you rest. It was meant to be a delight; but the Pharisees had turned it into a straitjacket.

Since his Father had blessed the Sabbath (Genesis 2:3), it was the most "natural" thing in the world for Jesus to bless and heal people on it. After all, his healing miracles were little foretastes of the glorious restoration that would take place on the final Sabbath day of resurrection. So, it is no surprise that he noticed a needy woman in the congregation that day. He couldn't really miss her while he was teaching during the service because she was incapable of standing up straight. For some eighteen years she had been severely disabled by a back deformity. Jesus called her over, laid his hands on her and freed her from the disability.

Imagine the scene as Jesus places his hands on the woman—probably on her bent back, don't you think? You can almost see his hands straightening it out. After all these years of being diminished in stature, she began to stand tall.

If you have ever known someone with a severe back deformity, you will find this a staggeringly moving moment. I think of a dear elderly lady in our congregation who had to turn and raise her head in order to speak to me, and who regularly received painful spinal injections to give her some relief. Would you not shed tears of joy to see Jesus place his hands on someone like that?

Not, apparently, if you were the president of this synagogue. He had invited Jesus to teach—but Jesus, not content with merely preaching God's word, *had worked!* The president stood up in front of the congregation and gave them a lecture on the spiritual dangers of the healing of suffering people on the Sabbath: *If you want Jesus to heal you, come back on a weekday!*

Jesus was full of compassion for this woman. But he was fierce in his response to the ruler and his friends. They were "hypocrites" (v 15). They condemned this woman for being healed on the Sabbath, but they had no hesitation about untying their donkey and leading it to get a drink of water before the synagogue service.

Sin is always inconsistent, and Pharisees exist all over the place. There is the religious variety, of course, as here. And there is the secular variety (our media can be lamenting the death of a pregnant whale and her unborn calf due to plastic pollution on one day while passionately advocating abortion rights the next). Sinners can never be consistent. But saints are called to be precisely that. And one area in which we should seek to be consistent is in "[calling] the Sabbath a delight" (Isaiah 55:13). To be like Jesus: to use it well. That has a knock-on-effect. It helps you to use the rest of the week well too.

There were at least two people in the service that day who called the Sabbath a delight. Jesus was one; the crippled woman became the other.

REFLECT

- Would it make any difference to how you live your week for the glory of the Lord if you called the Sabbath a delight?

RESPOND

THURSDAY

THE QUESTIONER WHO MISSED THE POINT

Luke 13:22-30

Have you ever had a tour of a historic site—perhaps the Tower of London, or the Gettysburg Battlefield, or Westminster Abbey—only for your guide to be interrupted by the words "I have a question"? For some of us, that moment quite often makes us cringe inside. The questioner may be a know-all who is embarrassing or a know-nothing who embarrasses themselves!

There is nothing new under the sun. Questioning voices were regularly heard in the crowds that gathered around Jesus on the road to Jerusalem. Here comes another:

"Lord, will those who are saved be few?" (v 23).

Jesus never answered *questions* without answering *questioners*. We usually find out what he thought of the questioner by the way he responded to the question. This is a case in point.

People love to discuss theology. Paradoxically, it even happens when you have a conversation about atheism with an atheist! If you are a "religious professional" (like me), it can get a bit wearing when you tell people what you do, only to have them give you their expert monologue on religion! Or be asked their self-assured problem questions, not dissimilar to this one: *Ok, Jesus, so are there going to be only a few people saved at the end of the day?*

Jesus' Jewish contemporaries by and large thought that at least most Jews would be saved—they were, after all, God's chosen people. But what did Jesus think?

Look at the first way Jesus answers the question.

He doesn't.

He "answers" the questioner by saying three things for the whole crowd to hear:

1. *That is not the question you should be asking* (v 24). *What you should be asking is, "Am I going to be saved?" So, make sure you come to me and get through the door that leads into the kingdom of God.*

2. *Make sure you "strive to enter" now, while you have the opportunity* (v 25). *One day it will be too late. The door will be shut.*

3. *Don't confuse having seen me and listened to me with coming to me* (v 26). Jesus had already taught in the Sermon on the Mount that belonging to him is not merely having contact with him or even doing miracles in his name. It is being known by him (Matthew 7:21-23). So, the question is not, "Did you know about me and were you in my presence?" It is, "Did you trust me and enter my kingdom?" *The question you should be asking,* says Jesus, *is not "How many will be saved?" but "Am I saved?"*

But then Jesus added, "People will come from the east and west, and from north and south, and recline at table in the kingdom of God" (13:29). Yes, many will be saved (see the vision in Revelation 7:9). But what good will it do you to know this if *you* are not saved?

When I was fourteen, on one cold Sunday night in January, I was walking home from church and slid on the ice.

As I caught my balance, a man wearing a dark coat appeared beside me. I saw him glancing down at the Bible in my hand. He looked up and stunned me with a question: "Are you saved, son? Are you saved?" How could he have known that that was what I wanted to be sure of more than anything in the world?

But did the man who asked Jesus the question want to be saved? Do you?

REFLECT

- We should never be more interested in theological questions than we are in knowing Jesus himself. How should that shape the conversations you have with other Christians or the way you approach the Bible?

RESPOND

FRIDAY

THE CROWD THAT NEEDED CHALLENGING

Luke 14:25-33

I think I heard sermons on these verses at least once a year when I was a teenager. And they appeared in many of the books I read—whether they were biographies of Christian heroes or books of teaching on the Christian life. Taking up the cross, counting the cost, making sacrifices, being willing to suffer—these were frequently repeated themes. When I left high school, one of the few openly Christian teachers gave me Dietrich Bonhoeffer's famous book *The Cost of Discipleship*. Who could forget its most famous sentence? "When Jesus calls a man, he bids him come and die."

But I can't remember when I last heard a sermon on 14:25-33. Books on the cost of discipleship appear infrequently. Perhaps once in a blue moon. At the same time, as the years have passed, only a minority of books have focussed on the meaning of the cross for the Lord Jesus or its significance for us.

Do you think, perhaps, that these two things stand or fall together? There is certainly a lot of talk about "discipleship" but not so much about the meaning of Jesus' death or about carrying the cross. There seems to be more emphasis on "being taught" than sacrificing, on doing rather than suffering, on knowing how to order your life better rather than being willing to go anywhere and do anything for Christ.

That, after all, is at first glance (and maybe tenth glance too!) a more attractive message. It is likely to draw more people into the Christian crowd.

At this point on the road to Jerusalem, Jesus himself was being followed by great crowds—at times numbering thousands (12:1).

We tend to be much more impressed by crowds than Jesus was. He made it clear that his focus was not on the number of his followers but on whether that number followed him without reservations. And here he makes it crystal clear what that means. In fact, he explains the *sine qua non*—the essential condition—for being a Christian. Without this, a person "cannot be my disciple" (14:26, 27, 33).

The principle he lays down is this: following him must have absolute priority in your life. In fact, if you don't hate father, mother, wife, children and your own life, you cannot be his disciple.

Notice that Jesus isn't saying that without this radical commitment you can still be a decent, but not a really great, disciple—he says that you can't be a disciple at all.

And if you have heard people say that "hate" here simply means "love less", forget it. It is much more radical than that. What Jesus is saying is that by comparison with your devotion to him, all other loves must seem like hate—and that includes your natural love for yourself. He is calling us to "die" to everything we count dear in our lives.

This is why he went on to talk about taking up the cross and following him. After his death, those words must have come back to the disciples with overwhelming force. He was asking them to be willing to do what he would first do for them.

If this is the case, no wonder we need to sit down and count the cost, because unless I am willing to have my whole life first deconstructed and then reconstructed by Jesus, I will never be his disciple.

Once again Jesus makes clear that following him—becoming a disciple, being a Christian—is an all-or-nothing business.

REFLECT

- Have you given yourself to Jesus? Only if you have will you be able to give up anything for Jesus. How do we see Jesus demonstrating this same cross-shaped commitment to us?

RESPOND

SATURDAY

THE GRUMBLERS

Luke 15:1-2, 11-32

The documentary was about a famous English composer. He was wonderfully talented. He was also an adulterer. A woman who knew him was interviewed and complained with some emotion: "Some people say _____ wasn't a Christian. But of course he was! He was a charming man."

This is make-believe Christianity.

Creating your own brand of Christianity is by no means only a contemporary phenomenon. But Jesus does not accommodate himself to others in this way. That was what frustrated, irritated and then eventually angered so many of the Pharisees and scribes. He did not fit into their preconceived ideas of what the Christ should be. And worse, he freely associated with "tax collectors and sinners"—the great unclean and unwashed who did not conform to the Pharisees' religious scruples. So, the Pharisees and scribes "grumbled, saying, 'This man receives sinners and eats with them'" (v 2).

They had obviously never read the Hebrew Bible carefully! From its third chapter onwards, it tells the story of the God who "receives sinners and eats with them"! That was what the annual feasts of the Old Testament calendar were all about: how God "receives sinners and eats with them"!

Thus they "grumbled" about Jesus. Being so self-assured that they were the only ones the Lord should be gracious to, it never crossed their minds that grumbling had been the national sin that had left rotting in the desert the corpses of their Exodus forefathers, who had failed to enter the promised land. Interestingly, food had been on their grumbling menu then too! They complained that they no longer had "the cucumbers, the melons, the leaks, the onions, and the garlic ... nothing at all but this manna" (Numbers 11:5-6). They had despised the bread from heaven then, and their descendants were despising the Bread from heaven still (John 6:33-35).

What has this to do with the parable of the Prodigal Son (in verses 11-32)? It is the reason why Jesus "told *them* [i.e. the Pharisees and scribes who grumbled] this [three-part] parable" (15:3).

In part three of this triptych, the prodigal is the "younger" of "two sons". This isn't a parable about just one lost son but about two. In parables (as in jokes) the punch line comes at the end. So, we shouldn't miss the point that while the prodigal son represents the tax collectors and sinners that Jesus received, the elder brother represents the Pharisees and scribes.

Why is that important? Because many Christians are also recovering Pharisees! So in some respects, you may be more like the stay-at-home elder brother than the younger prodigal. True, you may have once been a father-despising, home-leaving rebel, returning to God from a pig sty in "the far country". But perhaps not. Perhaps you have stayed at home in the church all your life. And yet ... and yet, in your relationship with the Lord there lurks in your heart an echo of the elder brother: "All these years *I've been slaving for you...*" (15:29, NIV). Are you harbouring a deep-seated sense that being a Christian is being a *slave*, rather than being a *son* of the loving Father?

Is there a remedy? Yes, the one that Jesus puts into the mouth of the Father in the parable: "All that is mine is yours" (v 31).

That is the joy of the gospel. God offers you everything he has in his Son. His Son now says to you, *Give me all that is yours—your sin, your shame, your suspicion of me, your fear of what following me will involve—give it all to me. Say to me, "All that is mine is yours" and I will say to you, "All that is mine is yours".*

Have you done that? It is time you did.

REFLECT

- How do your actions and attitudes reveal whether you are slaving for God or living as a beloved child of God?

RESPOND

THE THIRD WEEK OF LENT

—

THE PATH OF DISCIPLESHIP

SUNDAY

Take up thy cross, the Saviour said,
If thou wouldst my disciple be;
Deny thyself, the world forsake,
And humbly follow after me.

Take up thy cross: let not its weight
Fill thy weak spirit with alarm;
His strength shall bear thy spirit up,
And brace thy heart and nerve thine arm.

Take up thy cross, nor heed the shame,
Nor let thy foolish pride rebel;
Thy Lord for thee the cross endured,
To save thy soul from death and hell.

Take up thy cross then in his strength,
And calmly sin's wild deluge brave;
'Twill guide thee to a better home;
It points to glory o'er the grave.

Take up thy cross and follow Christ,
Nor think till death to lay it down;
For only those who bear the cross
May hope to wear the glorious crown.

(Charles W. Everest, 1814-1877)

MONDAY

THE APOSTLES WHO
WANTED TO GROW

Luke 17:5-10

"**I**ncrease our faith," the apostles asked Jesus (v 5). That's an interesting way to put it, isn't it? Surely we either have faith or we don't have faith? Or does it come in different sizes? After all, Jesus spoke about "little faith" and "great faith". Here he speaks about mustard-seed-size faith that can uproot trees and replant them in the sea. What even is faith?

Please don't misunderstand this next statement, because it may help you: *there is no such thing as "faith"!*

Faith is not a thing, a commodity, that is given to you or a substance infused into you, so that once you receive it, you have "got" it. It is not a spiritual kryptonite that you can get in small, medium, large and extra-large doses. No, there is no such "thing" as faith. There are only believers—people who trust in Christ.

What, then, is meant by "great" or "little" faith, or mustard-seed-size faith? These are ways of describing the extent to which our trust in the Lord is commensurate with the greatness of his person and the certainty of his promises; for the strength of faith is not found in my trusting but in his trustworthiness. Faith takes its character and strength not from its subject (the believer) but from its object (the Lord and his promises). This is why our spiritual forefathers used to say that little faith gets the same Saviour as great faith, but it may not get his greatness.

Jesus' statement about throwing mulberry trees around is hyperbole. (He never did that himself.) It is like his language in Matthew 17:20, where he says that faith as small as a mustard seed can move mountains. Both he and the apostles either climbed or walked round mountains—they didn't remove them, even momentarily, for convenience and speed of travel!

But why follow this statement about faith with a description of the servant who does only what is his duty?

Perhaps Jesus recognised a tendency many of us have—to become so impressed by what God does through our faith that we begin to think of that faith as a personal contribution we have made that deserves his reward. But the truth is that while faith actively engages in the service of God, it contributes nothing to what he accomplishes but only benefits from it.

You may have been taught as a young Christian that "faith" is an acronym of "Forsaking All I Take Him". That description is not the whole story; but it is always true. And forsaking all means recognising that faith has no power in itself. It contributes nothing to our justification. It rests and acts in Christ alone. It is always the empty hand that receives. Faith is always receptive of God's promises and never a contributor to his actions.

Thus, the man or woman of faith contributes nothing to Christ, receives everything from Christ and does everything for Christ. Faith is always a servant, never the master.

There is, however, another dimension in our Lord's teaching on servants. In the light of his words here, it may surprise us. Indeed, it *ought* to surprise us. One day he will say to his servants, "Well done, good and faithful servant ... Enter into the joy of your master" (Matthew 25:21, 23).

On that day you will not be likely to respond, "Yes, it was rather well done, wasn't it?" No—you will say, perhaps through tears of joy, "Lord what did I ever do to deserve your commendation?"

And he will say, *My child, even my "well done" is all of my grace.*

REFLECT

- *When I see by faith that I am nothing and Christ is everything, then I can receive by faith everything he has for me.* If Christ were to say to you, "Well done..." what do you think your instinctive response would be?

RESPOND

TUESDAY

THE ONE OUT OF TEN

Luke 17:11-19

A missionary surgeon once showed me a photograph of one of his patients—a man who had undergone amputations because of the ravages of leprosy on his body. The contrast between his body and his face was stunning. He had the most amazing smile I think I have ever seen. My friend said, "He says, 'I am so glad I had leprosy, otherwise I would never have met the Lord Jesus'".

Perhaps he was not the first person to say that. Many centuries before, in the borderland between Galilee and Samaria, a leper could likewise be heard "praising God with a loud voice … giving [Jesus] thanks" (v 15, 16).

Leprosy in the Bible is a generic term for a wide variety of conditions. It could refer to mould in a house, to infections of the skin or to the severe condition that we today call "leprosy". It was carefully regulated by the Mosaic Law (which included not only moral directives but health regulations too). Contracting leprosy meant immediate isolation from social life. It was the only way to protect the community. The leper had to leave home and family, spouse and children, work and pleasure. It was a living death unless the disease went into remission. In Jesus' day the only "isolation ward" available was removal from the village (described in Leviticus 13:45-46). The only society available to the leper was other lepers.

This little leprous band had probably heard from others how Jesus had healed leprosy (5:12-14; 7:22). So, they shouted over the gap, "Jesus, Master, have mercy on us" (17:13).

If you read Luke's Gospel from the beginning, you'll notice that mercy is an important theme (see 1:50, 54, 58, 72, 78). It features again and again. It was part of the punchline in the parable of the Good Samaritan ("the one who showed him mercy", 10:37). Somehow these lepers had heard that Jesus was merciful. He never refused a cry for mercy.

But Jesus' miraculous cures were not simply acts of mercy. They were signs that the kingdom of God had come (7:22) and that its King, Jesus, was reversing the effects of sin in people's broken and diseased lives.

The only people who could legally declare a leper "clean" (healthy) were the priests (hence Jesus' instruction in 17:14; see Leviticus 14:1-32). But while the priest could *declare* a leper clean, he could not *make* them clean. In addition, he could not show *mercy* to a leper; he had to banish them. It was not that the priest was evil; he applied the law. It was not that the law was evil; it banished lepers to protect the community, because it had no power to heal them.

The curse of leprosy with its terrible effects and the powerlessness of the priest and the law to save the leper, were stark realities. But they also served as a kind of dramatic parable of the human condition, and the powerlessness of the law to change it, even if it sought to control and regulate it.

What good news it must have been for these lepers to learn that Jesus was not only merciful but that he had the power to heal leprosy!

That is also good news for all of us. Jesus has come to be a "merciful ... high priest ... to make propitiation for the sins of the people" (Hebrews 2:17). He came to deal with the leprosy of our sin, guilt, shame and separation from God. What the law could not do because of our sin, God has done for us in Jesus Christ (Romans 8:3-4).

At the beginning of the story ten lepers "stood at a distance" (17:12). At the end, nine former lepers still stood at a distance. Only one praised God and returned to "[fall] on his face at Jesus' feet, giving him thanks" (v 16).

Does a ten per cent rate of thanksgiving shock you? But, then, when were you last thankful to Christ, and for what?

REFLECT

- When did you last fall "at Jesus' feet, giving him thanks" because of what he has done for you? Why not spend some time doing that now?

RESPOND

WEDNESDAY

THE INTERROGATORS

Luke 17:20-37

If you were given a blank card and asked to list the three central themes of Jesus' ministry, what would you write?

If it were me, the kingdom of God would have to be one of them. The phrase appears about forty times in Luke's Gospel alone. Jesus preached about the kingdom of God. He taught his disciples to pray daily that it would come.

But what, exactly, is the kingdom of God? When and how does it come? Has that question ever puzzled you? If so, you are not the first! It was a big question also for the Pharisees. And, since Jesus preached about it so often, one day some of them asked him directly, *When is the kingdom coming?*

Is this another question designed to trip up Jesus? Perhaps not. But even so, you'll notice that Jesus begins his reply with a couple of negatives. They both assume that the Pharisees who asked the question were at best muddle-headed in their expectations. They held to what we might call the "Big Bang Theory" of the coming of the kingdom of God: spectacular displays of power and glory ("signs to be observed", v 20). Later, in private, Jesus further explains this to his disciples. They should not be *deceived* about how the kingdom comes *now*, and they should not be *unprepared* for the day when it will be consummated *in the future* (17:22-37).

But what about the kingdom itself? Jesus tells the Pharisees, "Behold the kingdom of God is in the midst of you" (v 21). The Authorized (King James) Version translates this as "within you", but that is misleading. It is not true that everyone has the kingdom of God within them—even Pharisees. Nor does Jesus ever speak about God's kingdom as something that enters us. No, we need to enter it. Remember the Pharisee Nicodemus? Jesus told him that without spiritual rebirth he would be incapable of seeing or entering the kingdom of God (John 3:3, 5).

Here in Luke 17, Jesus says that the kingdom the Pharisees needed to enter has already arrived; it is in their very midst! What, then, could this kingdom be? How has it come near them? Answer: Jesus is the King; wherever he is reigning, the kingdom of God is present. The kingdom is among them; indeed, its King is standing right in front of them!

This explains why Jesus' teaching about his kingdom refers to both the present and the future. It *has already come*, and it *is still coming*. That is why those who already belong to the kingdom are taught to pray "your kingdom come" (see Matthew 5:3, 10; 6:10). The reign of Jesus Christ, which has been inaugurated by his presence on earth, will one day be consummated by his return in glory. Then "the kingdom of the world [will] become the kingdom of our Lord and of his Christ" (Revelation 11:15).

To be in this kingdom means to have entrusted yourself to King Jesus as your Saviour and to have received his pardon. The citizens in this kingdom are members of the ultimate royal family.

Jesus did not say to Nicodemus that unless a *Pharisee* is born again, he cannot enter the kingdom of God (John 3:3, 5). No, he said that unless *anyone* is spiritually reborn, he or she will never be able to recognise the King, abandon himself or herself to his reign and enter his kingdom.

That "anyone" includes you.

REFLECT

- Have you seen and entered the kingdom yet? If so, when was the last time you prayed "your kingdom come, your will be done"? Is there anything stopping you from praying that now?

RESPOND

THURSDAY

THE KINGDOM INFANTS

Luke 18:15-17

In the Hebrew Calendar, the Day of Atonement (Yom Kippur) was the one day in the year when the high priest could go into the holiest place in the Jerusalem Temple to offer a sacrifice for the sins of the people. When he came out to the people, he could pronounce again the blessing of peace: the face of God was turned towards them and the *shalom* of God granted to them for another year (see Numbers 6:4-6).

But the temple was in Jerusalem—too far for many to travel for Yom Kippur, especially if they had young children. And in any case, space was limited. It seems that out of this background a tradition developed: on the evening of Yom Kippur families would go to their local rabbi and ask for his blessing on them and on their children.

Perhaps that was the background to this scene; some parents were bringing their children to Jesus for his "touch" on their lives (18:15). The disciples wanted to turn them away. We can only guess why. Perhaps they were tired of people crowding Jesus; perhaps they thought he had more important things to do than to fuss around children, or they just wanted to have dinner. Jesus' reaction is well worth reading very carefully. He said three things:

1. Let the children come to me; don't stand in their way.
2. To such children belongs the kingdom of God.
3. If you don't receive the kingdom of God like a child, you will not enter it.

There's a lot going on here that we need to probe.

First, the word Luke uses for "children" means young children—infants. Luke had already used it of John the Baptist when he was still in Elizabeth's womb (1:41, 44).

Second, what Jesus said may have shaken the disciples. Far from thinking these youngsters were unimportant and to be ignored, he said, "To such belongs the kingdom of God" (18:16). Notice what Jesus is saying here. He says that the kingdom of God belongs *to these particular infants* and others like them.

Then, third, having spoken about these children, he goes on to speak about everyone ("whoever", v 17), using the children as an illustration. The only way to enter the kingdom of God is by *receiving* it—just as these little children have received it, as a free and gracious gift. Now he is saying something similar to his earlier words to Nicodemus. He needed to be born again, born from above, if he were ever to see and enter the kingdom. Poor Nicodemus—he wondered how he could do that! He didn't "see" that it was a sovereign gift from God.

Does this mean that Jesus is saying that all children receive his kingdom blessing? No—only "such as these"—that is, children whose parents were bringing them deliberately to him for the blessing of the kingdom's King. These parents looked to Jesus—not to the rabbi or even the high priest—to pronounce his kingdom blessing on them. It was an act of faith in the Lord Jesus. And he pronounced this blessing: "to such belongs the kingdom of God" (v 16).

If you're a parent, make sure you do what these mums and dads did—take your children to Jesus for his kingdom blessing: commit them to him in prayer. And, yes, let them know that you have done that, and teach them how to respond to him in faith and love.

REFLECT

- If Jesus loved little children, and wanted them to come to him, shouldn't you love them too? He still does! Spend time praying for children in your church family.

RESPOND

FRIDAY

THE RICH BUT SAD RULER

Luke 18:18-30

Many Christians—perhaps yourself included—read the Gospels as though every word has been spoken directly to themselves, when in fact the words were spoken to others.

But very few make this mistake when they read the words in verse 22: "Sell all that you have and distribute to the poor"! In this instance we are very clear: "Jesus said that to the rich ruler, not to me!"

Does that mean, when we read this story, that we are let off "scot-free"? (Where did *that* expression come from?!) Well, let's watch and listen.

Jesus' journey to Jerusalem has been punctuated by people asking him questions. Today it is a synagogue leader who is distinguished by the fact that he is rich. We don't discover that until the encounter is over; but it was probably fairly obvious.

The ruler addresses Jesus as "Good Teacher" and asks what to do to inherit eternal life (v 18).

Jesus responds with a question of his own that must have stopped the man in his tracks: *Only God is good. Is that what you mean when you call me "good"?* He then proceeds to de-construct him spiritually before his own eyes:

Jesus: *You want to know the way to eternal life? Let's begin with the commandments about adultery, murder, theft, bearing false witness, honouring parents.*

Rich ruler: *I have observed all of these since I was young!*

Do you see what Jesus has done already? The answer lies not in what he says but in *what he hasn't said.* These five commandments come from the second part of the law, which deals with how redemption impacts our relationships with other people. Jesus has not yet said anything about commandments one to four, which have to do with our relationship to God; and he has also omitted number ten, which has to do with coveting. This is what eventually undoes the man.

The fact is that if he had realised the full force of the first four commandments, he would not so quickly have said that he had kept commandments five through nine! And he would have realised that commandment ten revealed that money was his real god. Only when you love the Lord with all your heart, soul and strength can you keep the command to love your neighbour as yourself! But in this man's case, the evidence of his unconfessed failure is that his possessions are bonded to his soul as if with superglue.

Jesus' surgical scalpel now cuts. It will wound; but without that wound there will be no healing—no eternal life. *Sell everything; give to the poor; come and follow me; I will give you eternal life,* says the Lord.

Sadly, the young man was incapable of doing this. He could not let go of his wealth. The superglue was too strong. He could not bring himself even to tell Jesus that he could not do it. The result? "He became very sad, for he was extremely rich" (v 23).

Simon Peter (as usual) voiced what the other disciples were probably thinking: *If this man—with so many obvious qualities—can't gain eternal life, how can anybody be saved?* It seemed impossible.

Peter was right. But Jesus replied, "What is impossible with man is possible with God" (v 27). He can dissolve the superglue of self and sin. The good news is that he can release us from bondage.

If only the young ruler had said, *Lord Jesus, I can't; will you help me and release me from my bondage?* No matter how much he felt he was "giving up" for Jesus, he would have received "many times more [than anything he gave up] in this time, and in the age to come eternal life." (v 30).

REFLECT

- A brief life of false wealth is a poor exchange for an eternity of true riches. Is there anything sticking to your soul with superglue? Are you prepared to ask Jesus to release you?

RESPOND

SATURDAY

THE BLIND BEGGAR

Luke 18:35-43

Beggars can be seen in most major cities in the world. What do you think about them? Do you react differently if you see a *blind* beggar? It probably isn't their fault that they cannot see.

Jesus has now reached the city of Jericho, only twenty miles or so from his journey's destination, where he encounters one such blind beggar. Luke doesn't tell us his name; but Mark does. He was Bartimaeus.

Crowds must often have passed where this man sat—it was en route to Jerusalem. He had chosen his begging pitch carefully. But somehow, his well-developed other senses must have alerted him to something different about the passing traffic. You can see him, face lifted up, eyes vacant, asking, *What's happening? Who's coming?* and hearing the words *It's Jesus of Nazareth!*

Did Bartimaeus tense up at these words, and did his mind go into overdrive? "Jesus of Nazareth"—he knew that name. Jesus' fame had reached even to his roadside pitch on the Jericho road. This was the man who healed the sick and gave sight to the blind. Could Jesus heal him?

He must have felt it was now or never—the only chance he would ever have. So, he started shouting, "Jesus, Son of David, have mercy on me!" (v 36).

Someone in front of him turned around. *Shut up!* he said. Others looked down at him and agreed: *Yes, shut your mouth!* It's heartbreaking to think of this poor, lonely blind man being shouted down.

But Bartimaeus was desperate. He shouted louder than he had ever shouted in his life, "Son of David, have mercy on me!" (v 39).

Jesus heard two things that arrested him. First, that voice rising above the crowd belonged to somebody who recognised his identity—he was indeed the promised Messiah, the descendant of David whose reign would bring *shalom.* But in addition, whoever this person was, he was asking for mercy—an appeal Jesus never refused. Someone knew they needed him!

Don't you want to cheer, or perhaps weep for joy, when you read Luke's next words: "Jesus stopped" (v 40)? What a moment! And then he "commanded him to be brought to him".

Pause for a moment and try to visualise the scene. This is what Jesus was like. And he is the same today as he was then. And he will be like this tomorrow, and every tomorrow (Hebrews 13:8). And he is like this *for you.* Jesus hears. Jesus stops.

But now comes a surprise. Jesus asks what may seem a strange question: "What do you want me to do for you?" (18:41). Bartimaeus wants to see.

You know the rest of the story. Bartimaeus had been given the spiritual vision to see who Jesus was, the faith to believe in what Jesus could do ("let me recover my sight"), and the courage to overcome the opposition he experienced and to cry, "Lord, have mercy".

"And immediately he recovered his sight, and followed him, glorifying God" (v 43). "Followed" here is not a metaphor, but it is a wonderful and deeply moving picture, isn't it? He had been blind, but now he could see; he was a beggar, and Jesus had given him what he begged for. Had he felt all along that if he received his sight, there would be only one thing he would want to do? Yes, follow Jesus.

Sometimes it takes only one person trusting in the Lord Jesus to impact an entire group of people. As the excited band of disciples made their way on to Jerusalem, did Bartimaeus in turn hear the occasional voice rise above the chatter of the crowd and say, *Look, isn't that the blind beggar? Is that Bartimaeus following Jesus?*

"And all the people, when they saw it, gave praise to God" (v 43). No wonder!

REFLECT

- Who do you know who is spiritually blind? Pray that they will see the kingdom of God, trust in Christ and become part of your church family—with the result that all the people will give praise to God.

RESPOND

THE FOURTH WEEK OF LENT

—

FRIENDS AND ENEMIES

SUNDAY

No more, my God, I boast no more
Of all the duties I have done;
I quit the hopes I had before,
To trust the merits of Thy Son.

Now for the love I bear his Name,
What was my gain I count my loss;
My former pride I call my shame,
And nail my glory to the cross.

Yes, and I must and will esteem,
All things but loss for Jesus' sake:
O may my soul be found in him,
And of his righteousness partake.

The best obedience of my hands
Dares not appear before thy throne;
But faith can answer thy demands
By pleading what my Lord has done.

(Isaac Watts, 1674-1748)

MONDAY

THE SMALL TAX MAN

Luke 19:1-10

Jesus' long journey to Jerusalem is now coming towards its end. Luke will soon erect some signposts on the way to tell us that the destination is almost in sight (19:11, "He was near to Jerusalem"; 19:28, "He went on ahead, going up to Jerusalem"; 19:41, "He drew near and saw the city").

This may shed some light on the story that Luke is about to narrate. In some ways it summarises the whole of Jesus' ministry. Perhaps that is why it seems to have captured Luke's imagination.

Of all the Gospel authors, Luke is the one who writes like a historian. He tells us right at the start that what follows is his research project. But here we can almost imagine him as a moviemaker: "He entered Jericho and ... behold, there was a man named Zacchaeus" (v 1-2). *Do you see him there? Yes, that little man up the tree. Let me tell you about him!*

But that's not quite where the focus is. Zacchaeus is not the central figure here. This is a story about Jesus. Luke is saying, *Look at the picture.* Yes, you see Zacchaeus. But Zacchaeus isn't looking back at you from the frame. No,

Zacchaeus is looking at Jesus. It is as if Zacchaeus is saying to us, *Look at Jesus. Do you see what he was like to me?*

What was there about Jesus that made a chief tax collector want to see him?

In occupied Palestine taxes were collected from the inhabitants and paid to the occupying Romans—minus the self-determined percentage made by the tax collector. A chief tax collector like Zacchaeus could take home a comfortable profit. It was hardly surprising, then, that he and his like were mentioned in the same breath as "sinners" (5:30). It was understandable that nobody would budge to let this little man get a better view of Jesus.

But no doubt, even in the underworld of tax collectors, news travelled fast and widely. One of their number had very dramatically become a disciple of Jesus (5:27). He had then thrown an "I've become a disciple of Jesus" party and invited all his friends to meet the Saviour (and presumably the only friends of a tax collector were… yes, tax collectors). No wonder Jesus' name was on the lips of the gossipmongers of the day as "a friend of tax collectors" (7:34). Plus, numbers of tax collectors were listening to Jesus preach (15:1). And he had even told a parable about a tax collector who was counted righteous by God and a Pharisee who was not (18:9-14)!

So, it is perhaps not surprising that Zacchaeus was intrigued, even acting completely out of character by climbing up a tree to get a better view of this Jesus. You can almost hear the catcalls of some of the people he had been fleecing. (*Trying to get a better view of our money bags, Shortie?*)

What Zacchaeus could never have anticipated was seeing a pair of eyes looking right into the tree, and their owner— yes, Jesus—inviting himself to his house!

Zacchaeus became a real believer—that is, a repenting believer. He was determined to go back down the road along which he had strayed from God, giving back fourfold what he owed, and giving away half of his goods to the poor.

That day salvation came to Zacchaeus's house. Yes, he was hidden up the tree. Yes, he was in an unlikely place. And yes, he was an unlikely candidate for conversion. But Luke narrates all this to tell us something about Jesus: "The Son of Man came to seek and to save the lost" (19:10). Jesus was seeking Zacchaeus. He knew where to look for him. And he found him.

He always does.

REFLECT

- Are there things that have gone wrong in your life that you need to put right now that you are a believer, as you walk back down the road of repentance? What truths in this passage will help you to do that?

RESPOND

TUESDAY

THE MULTITUDE ON THE ROAD

Luke 19:28-48

Jesus is now near Bethany, only a couple of miles from Jerusalem. This time next week his journey will be over. He will spend Passover week staying with his friends Martha, Mary and Lazarus, and walking into Jerusalem on a daily basis. But already the many-thousands-strong crowd of pilgrims is making its way into Jerusalem.

Some details in the events that follow may seem a little enigmatic. Jesus tells two of the disciples to go into the village, where they will find a colt that has never been broken in. They are to untie it. If asked what they are doing, they are to give the simple reply, "The Lord has need of it" (v 31). The arrangement had probably been made well in advance.

Seated on the colt, Jesus now rides into Jerusalem surrounded by "the whole multitude" of pilgrim crowds, including many of his own disciples who have presumably met up on the way (v 37). Their excitement is palpable. They begin to chant the words of a psalm associated with Passover: "Save us, we pray [Hosanna], O LORD ... Blessed is he who comes in the name of the LORD" (Psalm 118:25-26). They are cheering him on as the long-awaited messianic King.

No wonder the Pharisees complain and tell him to rebuke his followers! How dare he accept this adulation! But silencing the disciples, Jesus responds, would be pointless; for if the crowds fell silent, the stones would begin to chant. However inadequately his disciples understand the significance of what is happening, they are right about who he is.

But then comes something unexpected. As the city comes into view, Jesus begins to weep. "Weep" means more than "cry". It implies deep, Jeremiah-like, painful, distressed tears (see Jeremiah 8:18-9:3). The Son of David echoes the pain of his forefather David over the rebellion and the death of his son Absalom (2 Samuel 15:30; 18:33). Jerusalem—the City of Peace—is blind to the One in whom its true peace lies.

The message of the Saviour's birth had rung out thirty years before to shepherds on the plains of Bethlehem, tending the lambs being reared for the coming Passover season (2:8-18). Now in Luke 19, many of the lambs born in Bethlehem were being driven into the temple precincts as Passover sacrifices. Among them—all the way from his birth in Bethlehem to the Jerusalem Temple—came the Lamb, whom God had nurtured and was now bringing into Jerusalem. He was the Passover Lamb, who would take away the sin of the world. After him there would be no one else to send. This was Jerusalem's last opportunity.

As if to signal this, Jesus entered the temple precincts and "drove out those who sold" (v 45)—the traders who profited from religion rather than served it. By passing no comment, Luke says a great deal. What authority Jesus has! For the moment (since all is under his Father's control) he remains untouchable. He is immortal until his work is done.

See Jesus' ability to ride on an unbroken colt while a vast, excitable and noisy crowd presses in on him. He comes with the authority of God's appointed King, as the true and last Adam (1 Corinthians 15:45, the first Adam being the one who lost the authority he was originally given over the animals).

See Jesus speak with authority to the Pharisees—for he comes as God's prophet to speak his last word.

See Jesus drive out the profiteers from the temple—for he comes to exercise the holy ministry of God's priest in the house of God.

He was the Messiah, the anointed One. He remains so. As prophet he continues to speak God's word to us through Scripture. As priest he has offered himself as a sacrifice to cleanse us from the guilt of sin and now intercedes for us. As king he comes to restore God's rule in our lives.

Yes, indeed, "Blessed is the King who comes in the name of the Lord!"

REFLECT

- What in particular strikes you as making Jesus worthy of your praise? Have you welcomed him and said, "Blessed is the King who comes in the name of the Lord"?

RESPOND

WEDNESDAY

THE CHIEF PRIESTS

Luke 20:1-8

WWJD. Do these letters ring a bell? Perhaps you remember those bracelets with the words, *What Would Jesus Do?*

To tell the truth, that isn't always the best question to ask, because you are not Jesus. But as we consider this passage, it really is helpful.

It is now the last week of Jesus' earthly life. He is in Jerusalem. Each day he goes up to the temple. The crowds gather round, and he teaches them, "preaching the gospel" (20:1). But look! Here come the chief priests and their retinue, presumably including Annas and his son-in-law, the current high priest Caiaphas.

The crowds must have parted like the Red Sea in Moses' day. Nobody becomes a religious leader without a "presence", whether attractive or otherwise.

In this case, it is undoubtedly the latter. Annas had been deposed from the high priesthood by Rome, and Caiaphas was appointed in his place. Hardly a shrewd decision, you would have thought, not least since the Jewish people continued to recognise the father-in-law as the true high priest.

And doubtless he continued to be the power behind the high priesthood!

But look again at the scene Luke is painting. On the one hand, see these two men, probably distinguished by their clothing, surrounded by their sycophantic entourage, marching up to Jesus, the carpenter of Nazareth in the northlands. Listen to their intimidating demand: *What authority do you have to be teaching here? Who gave it to you?* In their minds the answers are *No authority at all* and *Nobody; you just took it.*

Watch Jesus, and listen to what he says.

We have already seen the wisdom of the adage "Why does a rabbi always answer a question with a question?" (Answer: "Why not?") Notice again how Jesus responds. It has a lesson to teach us.

1. Jesus is asked a very direct question.
2. But Jesus does not give a direct answer.
3. Instead, Jesus asks a question of his own.

That second point will surprise a Christian who believes that faithful witnesses always answer every question they are asked and do so as directly and as fully as possible. After all, isn't that what 1 Peter 3:15 implies? (Look it up!)

Apparently, Jesus didn't think so. Perhaps he was thinking of Proverbs 26:4-5. (Look that up too; you may need to read the verses twice!)

We see once again that Jesus didn't just answer *questions*; he answered the *questioner*. Sometimes there is a big difference.

The chief priests were trying to make Jesus incriminate himself. They didn't expect him to respond with a question *they* couldn't answer without incriminating themselves! His question revealed their false motives, their sinful hearts and their inconsistency. How the crowd must have loved seeing the chief priests speechless for once!

What is the takeaway for us from this interchange?

Well, first it is to admire Jesus! But then we need to learn how to imitate him. Jesus didn't cast his pearls before pigs who would trample them and him. He taught us not to make that mistake either (Matthew 7:6). We need to learn to recognise pigs, wolves, and false sheep, and deceptive and deceitful inquisitors. We must listen to questioners, not just their questions. Rather than fall into their verbal traps, we need to learn how to respond in a way that silences them in their inconsistency. So always ask yourself not only "What is the answer to this question?" but also "Why is this person asking it?"

In other words, "What would Jesus do?"

REFLECT

- Do you know people who try to entrap you as a Christian? How can Jesus' example help you?

RESPOND

THURSDAY

THE SPIES ON A MISSION

Luke 20:19-26

My host's voice had been warm, cultured and welcoming when he spoke to me off-air about the interview on his radio programme. But now that we were on air, it suddenly became sharp, antagonistic, threatening and accusatory. He snarled out an opening question that was clearly intended to embarrass and confuse me.

He must have thought he had made a palpable hit—I suspect the same question had brought him a good deal of success in the past!

Amazingly, in the providence of God, I found myself breathing a quiet "Thank you, Lord", for the interviewer had touched on a theological issue with which I was intimately familiar. In fact, I suspected that if he had known what I knew, he would never have asked the question! So I phrased my response in a questioning way (rabbi style!): "Well, you'll know where that view originated, I suppose?" I was almost certain the interviewer would not know the answer. He didn't—and was flustered because he now had to adopt the pose of a learner rather than an intimidator. As it happened, the answer undermined all his motives in asking his original question.

On that occasion I was, to borrow some words from an old translation of Genesis 39:2, "a lucky fellow"! We're not always in that position. But all I had done was learn a lesson from Jesus.

Following the chief priests' earlier failure to entrap our Lord, another wave of attacks was now being launched. Some spies came, feigning sincerity with a three-fold compliment: "Teacher, we know that you speak and teach rightly, and show no partiality, but truly teach the way of God" (20:21).

They were lying through their teeth. If they had believed a fraction of what they had said, they would also have known that Jesus saw right through their façade! But having flattered him to their own satisfaction, they now twisted in the knife: *Is it lawful to pay taxes to Caesar, or not?*

You can almost hear them adding, as though they were hotshot lawyers in a TV trial scene, *Just answer the question "yes" or "no"!* (Incidentally, always beware questioning in that form because it often commits the logical fallacy known as *tertium non datur*—as though there is no third possibility.)

The question was loaded. Answer "yes" and Jesus' loyalty to Israel was in question and his reputation among ordinary people destroyed. He would be portrayed as an enemy of the people. But answer "no" and he would be summoned before the Roman authorities for treason. It was a lose-lose situation for Jesus.

Except for the fact that Jesus is wiser than his enemies.

His response is brilliant: *Does anyone have a denarius they can lend me for a moment? I promise I'll give it back!* He holds it up and asks, "Whose likeness and inscription does it have?" (v 24). The right answer is, of course, Caesar's. You can almost hear the spies' brains forming the words *Got him!* There was no way out for Jesus now… But no! Jesus continues: *Then give to Caesar what is Caesar's; but give to God what is God's.*

Do you get it? The spies did because they were silenced. Why? Because they knew Genesis 1:26-27. They had challenged Jesus at a political level. He was challenging them at a much deeper, more ancient, more personal level. They were made as God's image, created to be like him in his holiness and love. Jesus says, in effect, *By all means let Caesar have the denarius if his likeness and inscription are on it. But only if you'll let God have what he has stamped his likeness on and written his inscription on—you.*

There are lessons to learn here. The first is that Jesus cannot be manipulated. The second is this: if, like him, we develop minds that are saturated with both the truth and wisdom of Scripture, we are less likely to be manipulated as well.

REFLECT

- Think back to a time when someone tried to make you look small because you are a Christian, or to manipulate the truth. How would having a big grasp of the gospel and the Bible have helped you respond?

RESPOND

TO SEEK AND TO SAVE

FRIDAY

THE POOR WIDOW

Luke 20:46 – 21:4

It had been a testing few hours for Jesus in the Jerusalem Temple, but every attack on him had failed. Now he was counselling his disciples to beware of religious leaders—in this case, the scribes. He exposed them with surgical precision. They were men who loved to have position and praise but would "devour widows' houses" (20:47). We encounter their heirs today in the guise of preachers who manipulate people to part with their savings.

How fitting, then, that at this point Jesus could see people coming into the temple with their gifts. They were heading either for one of the side rooms where donations were received or perhaps to one of the trumpet-shaped receptacles where gifts could be deposited.

Perhaps the size of the gifts of the rich was made fairly obvious by the noise of their coins hitting the side or bottom of the offering boxes. Perhaps a group of idle Jerusalem boys were playing "Guess the offering" as they heard the "pings" or "clunks" the coins made.

But Jesus was watching one person in particular—"a poor widow" (21:2). Luke admired this about Jesus: he noticed and cared about the weak and disadvantaged. (The word "widow" appears more than twice as often in Luke's Gospel as in the other three combined.)

As Jesus watched, he noticed what the widow put in. Perhaps he saw her hand move only twice and scarcely heard the two tiny sounds as the coins dropped in. But he noticed something else that was even less obvious to others: something about her, the way she looked, or—who knows—perhaps the tears in her eyes. The Saviour knew that this woman had given everything she had.

Think of that. Do you know how much is left in this week's housekeeping budget? Or how much is in your wallet? Or whether you need to worry about the amount on your credit cards? If making sure that ends meet is a concern for you, you are probably in a better position to imagine what it was like for this widow to part with her two copper coins. And if it's not—if all your bills for the month are covered, if you have no debts to pay and there is still cash in your wallet—do you ever think of emptying your wallet into the church offering? Think about that this Sunday!

Or, when you read this passage, do you see it through tinted lenses that delude you into thinking that it was ok for this widow to give all she had because it didn't amount to much anyway?

Jesus' point was that she gave everything she had and kept back nothing. By his calculus she gave more than all the rich people who had put their gifts into the treasury. They gave out of an abundance—they still had plenty. They thought of giving in terms of what would still be left for themselves. She thought of it in terms of giving everything she had to the Lord even if she had nothing left for herself. Plus, she was a widow—there was no backstop for her.

Did Jesus, perhaps, raise his voice a little? Did he make sure that everyone heard him say, "Truly, I tell you, this poor widow has put in more than all of them" (v 3)? Did she become aware that Jesus was watching her? Did she see love written all over his face? If so, it would be all the reward and comfort she would ever need. That look would have been worth a fortune to her.

The real issue isn't ultimately about money, is it? It's about the heart. But too often our money sticks to our heart.

It's wonderful that Jesus noticed this widow. If anything, it's even more wonderful that he saw someone give everything she had to the Lord; for this week would end with him giving everything he had as well.

In that respect, in her own small way, this dear widow was Jesus-like.

REFLECT

- When you became a disciple of Jesus, you gave him all you are and have. But have you gradually been taking it back? What difference does it make to remember that Jesus gave everything he had for you?

RESPOND

SATURDAY

THE BETRAYER

Luke 22:1-6

Passover was imminent, and Jesus' enemies needed to act quickly, before the feast. Otherwise they would sully their celebrations. But how could they stage-manage his downfall without creating a riot among the crowds of pilgrims?

The spiritual blindness of these men is terrifying; their hypocrisy screams at us. But now the means to solving their conundrum presents itself from within Jesus' own disciple band—indeed, in the person of its trusted treasurer.

There is both a simplicity and a terrible gravity about Luke's statement: "Then Satan entered into Judas called Iscariot, who was of the number of the twelve" (v 3). A satanic indwelling. Of course, in ancient times God had promised that the serpent who had deceived Eve and led Adam into sin would bruise the heel of the Saviour (Genesis 3:15). Now that time had come. God was keeping his longest-standing and most-costly-to-keep promise.

Yet Judas could never have said, *I was forced to betray Jesus against my will*. He always had "free will". But, like us, he was "free" to choose and act only in keeping with his character—and, in his case, it had become profoundly warped, and now provided a landing ground for Satan. Unlike the other eleven disciples, Judas had never been inwardly cleansed (John 13:10).

Judas had been given amazing privileges. Early in Jesus' ministry, the Lord had called him to be an apostle (6:13-16). Judas had now been with him for three years, watching him and listening to him. He had been part of the small band of brothers who had witnessed and participated in Jesus' power-releasing ministry, beating back the kingdom of darkness (10:1-20). How could he possibly betray his Lord?

It can happen. Jesus had earlier warned his disciples that it was possible to call him Lord, do mighty works in his name, and even cast out demons—yet not truly be his (Matthew 7:21-23). The author of Hebrews would later give a description of people who sound uncannily like Judas. Even though they have "been enlightened... tasted the heavenly gift ... shared in the Holy Spirit, and ... tasted the goodness of the word of God and the powers of the age to come" (Hebrews 6:4-5), they fall away. They turn out never to have been "clean" (John 13:10).

For Judas, it seems falling away may have begun with a temptation related to money. He had been made the group's treasurer and entrusted with the disciples' finances. Even when he went to betray Jesus, some of his fellow apostles thought he was en route to engage in mercy ministry (John 13:29). But his hand was in the bag rather than guarding and sharing its contents. When Mary had lovingly anointed Jesus at the beginning of the Passover week, Judas had complained that the perfume could have been sold and the money given to the poor (John 12:4-5). The desire for "other things" was choking the good seed of the word of Christ (Mark 4:19). And now, for thirty pieces of silver, he would finally hand his Master over to those who were bent on destroying him. Judas was a living embodiment of one of Jesus' earlier parables: he was like a house swept clean of one demon but which had never been filled with the "furniture" of the gospel. Now the devil himself had flooded his heart. In his case, truly "the last state of that person is worse than the first" (11:24-26).

This is the one encounter on the path to Calvary where there is no longer an encounter. Jesus will soon be absent from Judas's life. He is already absent from his affection. What a warning sign Judas is to us to make sure that what begins as small, and perhaps seems to us only to be momentary spiritual backsliding, is brought to Christ for forgiveness.

The only way to do that is to make sure that you hide nothing from him and that you live in his presence.

Judas didn't.

REFLECT

- Is there anything you're hiding from Jesus? Bring it into the light of his presence now. Then read 1 John 1:7 and rejoice.

RESPOND

THE FIFTH WEEK OF LENT

—

TOWARDS THE CROSS

SUNDAY

Christ calleth yet: at last shall I not heed?
How long shall I refuse the grace I need?
While pleasure fades, and time's swift moments fly,
Still shall my soul in mortal peril lie?

Christ calleth yet: alas, this stubborn heart!
I feared his yoke, shrank from the nobler part;
God and my soul how oft have I betrayed!
He draws me still: rise, heart, be not afraid.

Yield to him now, once and for ever yield;
Make Christ thy portion, and his grace thy shield.
What though the world its pleasures still display?
Christ calleth yet: O heart, do thou obey!

(Gerhard Tersteegen, 1697-1769
Translated by Howell E. Lewis, 1860-1953)

MONDAY

THE MAN WITH THE JAR

Luke 22:7-23

Jesus had been going to Jerusalem, probably every year, since he was twelve (2:41-42). When you go on holiday to the same place twenty years in a row, you get to know people. So, there is probably nothing "supernatural" about the instructions that Jesus gave Peter and John: to go into the city, where "a man carrying a jar of water will meet you. Follow him" (22:10). In all likelihood, Jesus had already arranged to have a quiet room where he could eat the Passover with the disciples.

In due course, the man led them to one of the most famous unidentified rooms in human history: the upper room. Perhaps it was in this very room that the disciples gathered on Easter Sunday, and on other occasions.

Did any of the disciples tell this man what Jesus had said about how much these arrangements meant to him? "I have earnestly desired to eat this Passover with you [the disciples] before I suffer. For I tell you I will not eat it until it is fulfilled in the kingdom of God" (22:14-15).

A sudden tragedy took place in a much-loved family in our church. It was a "whole-church moment". We all felt the situation deeply. The following Sunday was due to be what Presbyterians call a "Communion Sunday"—when we would celebrate the Lord's Supper. As it happened, these words of Jesus were in the passage planned for the sermon.

The communion table was covered in white linen, on which lay the communion bread and wine. The elders would then take them to the congregation, seated, as it were, at one vast table. In this acted parable, the gospel would be proclaimed not only by hearing it from God's word but also by seeing and tasting it, and offering it to one another when we passed the gospel symbols of the bread and wine to each other.

I remember longing for that Sunday morning to come. My heart had been full of the grief I felt for this family. I wanted so much for our entire church family to be seated together at the Lord's Table. I think I caught a glimpse, for the first time, of what these words, on which I was to preach, must have meant to Jesus himself.

The significance of the annual Passover celebration was inscribed on the soul of our Lord Jesus. He had shared in it for as long as he could remember, first in Nazareth and then in Jerusalem. The nation to which he belonged had been created and shaped by it. Even more so, his own life and ministry were defined by it; for he was "the Lamb of God, who takes away the sin of the world" (John 1:29). Luke himself had earlier noted that on the Mount of Transfiguration, Jesus had discussed with Moses and Elijah his "departure, which he was about to accomplish at Jerusalem" (9:31). The Greek word Luke used, translated "departure", is *exodus*.

By his death and resurrection, Jesus was to lead his people out of bondage, not to the Pharaoh of Egypt but to Satan and sin. Every previous Passover had pointed to this Passover, like a shadow of the reality. They all pointed to the cross, to the real and final exodus that would come through the shed blood of the Lamb of God, sacrificed for the sins of the world (John 1:29).

Every time that Jesus had tasted the bitter herbs, eaten the Passover lamb and chewed the unleavened bread, the meals had all pointed forwards to this Passover. Now, this week, he would experience the bitterness of sin, would become the sacrificial lamb, and would give his life as bread for the world.

REFLECT

- Do you long for the Lord's Supper? Why, or why not? Whenever you receive the Lord's Supper, remember: "Christ, our Passover lamb, has been sacrificed. Let us therefore celebrate the festival, not with the old leaven … of malice and evil, but with the unleavened bread of sincerity and truth" (1 Corinthians 5:7-8).

RESPOND

TUESDAY

THE SELF-DECEIVING APOSTLE

Luke 22:31-38

The oldest promise in the Bible was that the serpent would bruise the heel of the offspring of the woman (but would, in the attempt, be bruised himself, Genesis 3:15). Satan had been attempting to do that from the beginning of our Lord's public ministry. And while Jesus had withstood his attack in the wilderness, "the devil" had only "departed from him *until an opportune time*" (4:13).

That time had now come with a vengeance. Satan had already captured the disciples' treasurer, Judas Iscariot. His next target stood right at the centre of the apostolic band; he had already functioned as their spokesperson and was destined to be their leader—Simon Peter.

Every time the names of the apostles are listed in the Gospels, Peter's comes first. The same is true whenever the "inner three"—Peter, James and John—are mentioned. Peter was the one who would "take the keys out of his pocket" on the Day of Pentecost and unlock the door into the kingdom of God through his gospel preaching (Acts 2:14-41). He would do the same for the Gentiles in the home of Cornelius (Acts 10:1-48). We do not need to think of Peter as the first "pope" (as the Roman Catholic Church does) to recognise that he was given a leading role in the building of the infant church. It is therefore not surprising that Satan focused his sights on destroying him. And so, Jesus has a special word for Peter.

In fact, Jesus warns all of the apostles that "Satan demanded to have you [plural]" (22:31). Indeed, on this score, Satan would act within a few hours at most. The disciples would be separated from their Lord, fleeing in fear of their own lives, like chaff easily blown away by the strong winds of fear.

But here, in verse 32, Jesus addresses Peter individually. He does so with deep emotion, signalled by the repetition of his name ("Simon, Simon")—just as he had earlier addressed Martha with similar emotion (10:41). Jesus switches from the second person plural ("Satan demanded to have [all of] you") to the second person singular ("I have prayed for you [Peter]"). Jesus has prayed especially for Peter, that his faith would not fail.

Sadly, Peter still had no more self-understanding than he had had earlier (9:28-36). He blurted out that he was willing to die for Jesus! But before the night was over, he had denied him three times (22:34).

That is why Jesus prayed for Peter in particular. All the others would run in fear, but they would not deny all knowledge of him. The road back from such a denial of the Saviour would be sore indeed. Even if Peter were restored, such desperate failure could easily haunt and paralyse him for the rest of his life. But notice how great a Saviour Jesus is. He prays that Peter's impending denial will not lead him to abandon the faith. More than that, Jesus gives him an exhortation full of hope for the future: "When you have turned again [turned back, repented or returned in faith], strengthen your brothers" (v 32).

It is surely one of the mysteries of God's providence in Peter's life—and also in our own lives—that without minimising his failure, God seemed to build it into the way he was preparing him to be an under-shepherd of his frail and sometimes straying flock. Our God is able to make all things work together for good for those who love him. So whatever we've done in the past, our lives need not be fruitless.

Failure is never final when Jesus prays for us.

REFLECT

- We are not preserved in the Christian life by our own courage, strength or wisdom, but only by the intercession of Jesus, without which none of us would be able to stand. How does that truth encourage or challenge you?

RESPOND

WEDNESDAY

THE ANGEL FROM HEAVEN

Luke 22:39-46

Many Christians have faced death with quiet submission. Why, then, did our Saviour Jesus not face his death in the same way? Instead he prayed, "Father ... remove this cup from me". Indeed, after an angel from heaven appeared, strengthening him (v 43), he prayed more earnestly. He was "in an agony ... and his sweat became like great drops of blood falling down to the ground" (v 44). It's hardly surprising that Martin Luther was moved to say, "No man feared death like this man!"

But what is the explanation? It lies in the contents of the "cup" which Jesus' Father was putting into his hands (v 42).

We also use the metaphor of a cup to describe certain experiences in life. But the Old Testament sometimes uses this expression in a more nuanced way. On several occasions the "cup" refers to the judgment of God on sinners. Here are two vivid examples:

> *Thus the LORD, the God of Israel, said to me: "Take from my hand this cup of the wine of wrath, and make all the nations to whom I send you drink it.*

*They shall drink and stagger and be crazed because
of the sword that I am sending among them." So
I took the cup from the LORD's hand, and made
all the nations to whom the LORD sent me drink
it: Jerusalem and the cities of Judah, its kings and
officials, to make them a desolation and a waste, a
hissing and a curse, as at this day.*

(Jeremiah 25:15-18)

*You will have your fill of shame instead of glory ...
The cup in the LORD's right hand will come around
to you, and utter shame will come upon your glory!*

(Habakkuk 2:16)

The language which the Gospel-writers use to describe
Jesus' response to the cup reflects this prophetic language.
Matthew and Mark both focus on Jesus' emotional experience ("My soul is very sorrowful, even to death", Matthew
26:38; he "began to be greatly distressed and troubled.
And he said ... 'My soul is very sorrowful, even to death'",
Mark 14:32-34). Luke, a physician by training, uniquely
brings out the impact of the Gethsemane experience on
Jesus' body. His sweat is like great drops of blood. (The
word Luke uses is *thrombos*, from which we get the medical
term "thrombosis"—a clotting of the blood in the circula-
tory system.)

Together, the Gospel accounts echo the physically and
emotionally violent atmosphere of the prophetic words.
Jesus is drinking the cup of the wrath of God; it causes him
to stagger. He will become an object at which people will
hiss (22:63; 23:11, 35, 36); he will die under a curse (Galatians 3:13). He staggers under the load, and experiences an
unparalleled sense of desolation. He tastes the shame as well
as the pain of crucifixion. And even *after* "there appeared to

him an angel from heaven, strengthening him", he remained "in an agony" and "prayed more earnestly" (22:43-44).

Jesus now sees with greater clarity than ever before the task he must undertake. If we are to be saved, he must be willing to be alienated from God, and to experience the covering up of his Father's face and the full force of these ancient descriptions of the cup of God's wrath. In Gethsemane he is staring into the cup in which the sting and poison of sin lies.

No wonder Alexander Whyte, the famous 19th-century Scottish preacher, said that once he had seen the Lord Jesus in glory, he would next want to meet the angel who came to strengthen him in Gethsemane. For this angel was the only witness on earth of the moment when our Saviour contemplated the agony he would endure for our sake.

REFLECT

- "But the anguish he endured, our salvation hath procured" (from the hymn "Jesus Christ is risen today"). Why was our salvation so costly, do you think? How does it make you feel to know that Jesus has borne the cost?

RESPOND

THURSDAY

THE TEMPLE SOLDIERS

Luke 22:47-53, 63-65

The betrayer was, in the darkest sense, a man possessed: "Satan entered into Judas" (22:3). Now we
see public evidence. Not content merely to inform against
Jesus—after all, Judas needed only to tell the authorities
that he would be in the Garden of Gethsemane—we see
him now leading men with blazing torches and members of the temple guard. And, yes, although it seems
almost beyond credibility, here too are the chief priests
and members of the Sanhedrin. They are creatures of the
night in every regard.

Jesus, however, does not see his life in merely horizontal,
historical terms, as though these men are acting entirely on
their own initiative. He sees the visible in the light of the
invisible. There is a yet more powerful and sinister enemy
at work: "This is your hour," he says to the mob; but it is
even more so the hour of "the power of darkness" (v 53).
He is now entering the final phase in his lifelong conflict
with the evil one.

The temple guard take Jesus to the official residence of
the high priest. We should take careful note of what they do.

They play a cruel game of "Blind Man's Buff" with him. In this case it is given an especially cynical twist—here they are playing "Blind Prophet's Buff": "Prophesy! Who is it that struck you?" (v 65).

Yet planted deep within these hours lies a variety of clues to how, and by whom, God's first promise of redemption in Genesis 3:15 will be fulfilled. Among them is the promise of Moses: "The LORD said to me … 'I will raise up for them a prophet like you from among their brothers. And I will put my words in his mouth, and he shall speak to them all that I command him'" (Deuteronomy 18:17-18).

Jesus was that prophet. But his own people did not believe him when he prophesied. And now they trivialise his ministry in their callous game. Pushing him around, slapping and beating him, they shout at him, *If you are really a prophet, tell us who is hitting you now!* They pour humiliation on him. No one comes to his defence.

Jesus stands before them, the Divine Seer, whom they blindfold. He is the one on whose lips are God's words, yet they slap him on the mouth. He is the prophet promised by Moses. But they are too blind to recognise him.

And they do not realise that, even in doing this, the prophecies concerning this prophet are being fulfilled:

> *The Lord GOD has given me the tongue of those who*
> *are taught, that I may know how to sustain with*
> *a word him who is weary. Morning by morning he*
> *awakens; he awakens my ear to hear as those who*
> *are taught. The Lord GOD has opened my ear, and I*
> *was not rebellious; I turned not backward. I gave my*
> *back to those who strike, and my cheeks to those who*
> *pull out the beard; I hid not my face from disgrace*
> *and spitting. (Isaiah 50:4-6)*

For Jesus the Prophet is also the Suffering Servant, whose portrait Isaiah painted so vividly. He is now drinking the cup he has taken from his Father's hands in Gethsemane.

And as we watch this happening, how ought we to respond? We stand in silence, in wonder, in faith—and worship.

REFLECT

- These events are simply another violent episode in human history—unless we understand what God was doing in them: "For our sake he made him to be sin who knew no sin, so that in him we might become the righteousness of God" (2 Corinthians 5:21). Re-read these verses in Luke, pausing periodically to remember that it was all for your sake.

RESPOND

FRIDAY

THE SANHEDRIN

Luke 22:66-71

Jesus has been demeaned and despised, beaten and slapped. There is worse to come, some of which Luke omits—John tells us in his Gospel that the actions of the temple guards were repeated and indeed intensified, as Roman Soldiers mocked him not only as a prophet but as a "king" (John 19:1-3). But now, as he is brought before the Sanhedrin, the ruling body of Israel, and its leading figures, the third dimension of Jesus' messianic ministry is on trial.

The temple guards have derided him as God's prophet, and the soldiers as God's king. Here he is mocked in his role as God's priest—whose task is to make a way for sinners into the presence of God—as the high priest of Israel charges him with blasphemy. Jesus himself will therefore be put to death—as though he were a priest's sacrificial victim.

Yet, in a wonderful way, the central message of the gospel is woven into these actions which are intended to destroy our Lord.

He is asked if he is the Christ. It is not the first time this question has been raised. John the Baptist himself sent people from his prison cell to ask if Jesus really were the Messiah

(7:19). The events John had expected would accompany the Messiah's coming had not materialised. No baptism with fire had come; the winnowing fork that John prophesied lay unused (Matthew 3:12). Had John made a mistake?

On the contrary. As Jesus' response showed, John needed to remember that his Hebrew Bible had painted a bigger picture of the Messiah. Yes, the day would come for the baptism with fire. But for now, the message was one of grace and restoration: "Go and tell John what you have seen and heard: the blind receive their sight, the lame walk, lepers are cleansed, and the deaf hear, the dead are raised up, the poor have good news preached to them. And blessed is the one who is not offended in me" (7:22-23).

The majority of the Sanhedrin's members, whether Pharisees or Sadducees (it was composed of members of both sects), and certainly the high priests Annas and Caiaphas, were offended by Jesus—enough to plot to destroy him. So they deserved no direct response to their demand: "If you are the Christ, tell us" (22:67). He had already told them by his lifestyle, his teaching and his mighty works. He knew their hearts well enough; their question lacked integrity. They were simply seeking to trap him. And so, he replied with dignity, "If I tell you, you will not believe, and if I ask you, you will not answer" (v 67-68). They must have realised that he saw right into their hearts.

But Jesus does not leave things there. He issues a word of warning to them. They may think they hold the power of life and death over him in the judgment they will soon pass. But all too soon, they will stand before "the Son of Man ... seated at the right hand of the power of God" (v 69), and they themselves will be judged. In condemning Jesus, they will condemn themselves.

How striking that in their fury they see clearly what Jesus' words imply—"Are you the Son of God, then?" Who else could claim this position of highest honour? *You are essentially admitting that yourselves!* responds Jesus.

How quickly they twist the evidence as if Jesus himself had said it. Outsmarted in their legal trickery, they now resort to sleight of hand: they condemn him and in mob-justice rush him to Pilate for Rome to pronounce the death sentence they desire.

In our mind's eye, beside Luke's word-painting of this dark scene, we should place Simon Peter's explanatory note: "For Christ also suffered once for our sins, the righteous for the unrighteous, that he might bring us to God" (1 Peter 3:18).

But all this meant nothing to most members of the Sanhedrin.

REFLECT

- In the words of Philip Bliss's hymn "Man of Sorrows", we have seen that "In my place, condemned he stood; Sealed my pardon with his blood". But does your heart respond with "Hallelujah! What a Saviour"? Spend time marvelling at and praising the Lord Jesus now.

RESPOND

SATURDAY

THE TRAPPED POLITICIAN

Luke 23:1-5; 13-25

The expression "15 minutes of fame" is said to have been inspired by words appearing in a programme for an exhibition of the works of Andy Warhol in Stockholm in 1968.

The photographer Nat Finkelstein claimed he was their originator. As a crowd gathered round Warhol, Finkelstein responded to his comment that everyone wanted to be famous: "Yeah, for about 15 minutes, Andy."

If Pontius Pilate ever craved fame—and presumably as a Roman governor he had some streak of ambition—he has certainly achieved it, and for more than 15 minutes. Now, every Sunday, Christians all over the world say in unison the words of the Apostles' Creed: "Jesus Christ ... suffered under Pontius Pilate".

Picture the scene: Passover is a nerve-wracking enough week for Governor Pilate. Jerusalem is flooded with Jews from throughout the empire and beyond. Tensions are high. It is early on Friday morning. Since Pilate fell asleep a few hours before, Jesus of Nazareth has been betrayed, arrested, abused, tried and condemned by the chief priests and the

Sanhedrin. Now, mob-like, they are in his courtyard demanding to see him.

The Sanhedrin had only limited power over life and death—in extreme cases, such as a Gentile entering beyond the outer court of the temple. But carrying out a death sentence for blasphemy—the charge of which they found Jesus guilty—was not in their power. They needed to find a different accusation against Jesus—one that would carry the death sentence: treason. Listen to the words on the charge sheet in verse 2:

1. "Misleading our nation"—a scarcely-veiled claim that he was stirring up rebellion.
2. "Forbidding us to give tribute to Caesar."
3. "Saying that he himself is ... a king."

Treason indeed! Pilate could be a cunning and indeed a vicious man, but he was no match for these snakes. He was cornered; his worst Passover nightmare was now a reality.

Pilate cuts to the chase by asking Jesus directly, "Are you king of the Jews?" "You have said so," Jesus replies.

John's Gospel indicates that the interrogation was more extensive than this. To his credit, Pilate reaches a decisive verdict: Jesus is not guilty! But then he plays his get-out-of-jail card: Jesus is a Galilean. Galilee is Herod's jurisdiction; so Pilate can shift responsibility.

But before long Jesus is back. Pilate again delivers the same verdict. But now he has devised a compromise which he offers—a physical scourging instead of a death sentence. But faced with Jewish religious leaders demanding the release of the insurrectionist called Barabbas and the crucifixion of Jesus, Pilate wilts—despite having all the authority of the Roman Empire behind him. He sets a murderer free and has Jesus sent off for crucifixion. So much for justice.

Yet, woven into this travesty of justice is the evidence of a higher justice. For here God will show himself to be just and the justifier of those who believe in Jesus (Romans 3:26). For how can we who are guilty be declared righteous in his sight? Only if Jesus, in his incarnation, becomes one with us as humans and a substitute for us as sinners in his crucifixion. He has come to take our place and be counted as guilty in our place. And so, within this single chapter of Luke's Gospel, Jesus is declared to be *not guilty* by Pilate, then by Herod, then by one of the dying criminals at his side, and finally (as we shall see later) by the very man who was in charge of his execution. And yet still he is condemned.

The innocent One is treated as the guilty One in order that the guilty ones may be treated as righteous ones. This is the heart of the gospel.

REFLECT

- Imagine you were the one being released from Pilate's prison: what would you resolve to do next? For the rest of his life Barabbas could say, "Jesus died instead of me". But the Christian can say, in a much deeper sense, "The Son of God ... loved me and gave himself for me"—and so "the life I now live in the flesh I live by faith" (Galatians 2:20).

RESPOND

HOLY WEEK AND EASTER SUNDAY

—

THE FINAL DESTINATION

SUNDAY

My song is love unknown, my Saviour's love to me;
Love to the loveless shown, that they might lovely be.
Oh who am I, that for my sake
My Lord should take frail flesh and die?

He came from his blest throne salvation to bestow,
But men made strange, and none the longed-for Christ
would know:
But oh, my Friend, my Friend indeed,
Who at my need his life did spend.

Sometimes they strew his way, and his sweet praises sing,
Resounding all the day Hosannas to their King:
Then "Crucify!" is all their breath,
And for his death they thirst and cry.

Why, what hath my Lord done? What makes this rage
and spite?
He made the lame to run, he gave the blind their sight:
Sweet injuries! Yet they at these
Themselves displease, and 'gainst him rise.

They rise and needs will have my dear Lord made away;
A murderer they save, the Prince of life they slay.
Yet faithful he to suffering goes,
That he his foes from thence might free.

In life no house, no home, my Lord on earth might have;
In death no friendly tomb but what a stranger gave.
What may I say? Heav'n was his home,
But mine the tomb wherein he lay.

Here might I stay and sing, no story so divine;
Never was love, dear King, never was grief like thine.
This is my Friend, in whose sweet praise
I all my days could gladly spend.

(Samuel Crossman 1624-1683, alt)

MONDAY

THE FOXLIKE KING

Luke 23:6-12

Pontius Pilate sent Jesus to Herod Antipas. He was the son of Herod the Great, who, enraged at the thought of a rival king, had ordered the massacre of Bethlehem's baby boys (described in Matthew 2:16-18). Antipas was probably the most capable of Herod's sons; but his ability was combined with moral degradation. In a moment of drunken bravado, he had offered his wife's daughter anything she wanted as a reward for the way she had danced. On her mother's instructions, she asked for the head of John the Baptist (Mark 6:21-29).

It is nauseating to read that when Pilate sent Jesus to him, Herod's heart skipped a beat with excitement. There had been a time when the very mention of Jesus' name had given him serious pause for thought—he believed that Jesus' miracles indicated that he must be John the Baptist back from the dead (Mark 6:16).

Not now, however: "When Herod saw Jesus, he was very glad, for he had long desired to see him, because he had heard about him, and he was hoping to see some sign done by him" (23:8).

So, with neither a sense of guilt or remorse for what he had done to John nor any compassion for the figure who stood before him exhausted and demeaned, Herod questioned the Lord Jesus. But Jesus had long ago spoken his last word to Herod Antipas: "Go and tell that fox, 'Behold I cast out demons and perform cures today and tomorrow, and the third day I finish my course'" (13:32). There would be no further message now, not even in response to Herod's insistent questioning. Thus was the ancient prophecy fulfilled: "He was oppressed, and he was afflicted, yet he opened not his mouth; like a lamb that is led to the slaughter, and like a sheep before its shearers is silent, so he opened not his mouth (Isaiah 53:7).

Herod is not left alone. The chief priests and their minions are there, baying for Jesus' blood (v 10). Now Herod himself and his soldiers join in the terrible scene: "Herod with his soldiers treated him with contempt and mocked him" (23:11). Here Jesus stands before them, "despised and rejected by men; a man of sorrows, and acquainted with grief (Isaiah 53:3).

But Herod was not finished. He had one final scheme to further demean this rival "king". "Arraying him in splendid clothing" (23:11), he sent him back to Pilate: behold "our King", indeed. And on that day, Herod Antipas and Pontius Pilate, who had been enemies, became friends (v 12). Sin is like that (see Romans 1:32). These two men had nothing in common except hatred of Jesus.

But notice how regal the bearing of King Jesus is. He accepts the verdict. He will bear man's judgment against himself because he knows it is God's judgment on those in whose place he stands. He knows that this is the only way in which he can save us.

Soon the early Christians would come to understand this: "Truly in this city [Jerusalem] there were gathered together against your holy servant Jesus, whom you anointed, both Herod and Pontius Pilate, along with the Gentiles and the peoples of Israel, to do whatever your hand and your plan had predestined to take place" (Acts 4:27-28).

In every cruel detail, it was all as God had planned. And in every cruel detail, it was all endured for us.

REFLECT

- God can weave even human wickedness into his sovereign plan of salvation. Have you seen that in your own experience in the past? How does that strengthen you to face trouble in the future?

RESPOND

TUESDAY

THE MAN FROM THE COUNTRY

Luke 23:26

God's ways are mysterious and often completely unpredictable. Only ignorance or arrogance (and perhaps a combination of both) would lead us to think that we can know exactly what he is doing in our lives, or exactly how he will work things together for our good (Romans 8:28). But it isn't only what God does that is so amazing; it is also *when* he does it. Both his ways and his timing are perfect.

Take Simon of Cyrene, who came from what is modern-day Libya. We meet him as he is walking into Jerusalem from the country. Had he made a pilgrimage from his home town to celebrate the Passover? The city was always crowded at Passover, but perhaps he had found accommodation in one of the surrounding villages. Who knows what thoughts were passing through his mind as he walked into the city on that Friday morning? Perhaps he was realising a lifelong ambition—Passover in Jerusalem.

But now, with no warning, Simon finds himself turned around in the opposite direction by a Roman execution squad. He is conscripted to carry the cross on which one of their three prisoners is to be crucified. The condemned man appears to have been so badly beaten that he can no longer carry it.

The cross—or at least the cross-beam—is placed on Simon's shoulder. He now walks the road to Calvary in the footsteps of Jesus.

Those who watched these events unfolding must have thought, *Tough luck! Just in exactly the wrong place at the wrong time.*

Perhaps Simon thought the same—at least at first. Luke says no more. It was enough for him to let the picture speak for itself. It is a dramatic representation of the words of Jesus that Luke had earlier recorded—if you are going to be Jesus' disciple, you need to take up the cross daily and follow him (14:27). Simon is an acted parable of what it means to be a Christian.

But Mark fills in an extra detail: "They compelled a passerby, Simon of Cyrene, who was coming in from the country, *the father of Alexander and Rufus*, to carry his cross" (Mark 15:21).

So how did Mark know who Alexander and Rufus were, and why would he mention this detail? Presumably because these two sons of Simon of Cyrene became Christians and were known to the early church. And could this be the same Rufus whom Paul describes in Romans 16:13 as "chosen in the Lord" and whose mother was "a mother to me as well"?

Think of it: if Simon's sons became Christians, and his wife, it seems likely that, in God's amazing providence, this man who was once forced to carry the cross of Jesus later carried that cross willingly, as he became a disciple of the crucified Christ.

It may be that a whole family circle was brought to faith in Christ—all because of this "chance" encounter on the road out of Jerusalem.

We should try to remember that daily. It is the story of how Jesus builds his church. One "chance" encounter leads to another. One person becomes a link in the chain that eventually leads someone else to faith in Christ. And it all might begin with someone who feels that he or she just happened to be in the wrong place at the wrong time. But in God's purposes, there is neither a "wrong place" nor a "wrong time"!

REFLECT

- Perhaps later today someone will "by chance" meet a Christian who is reading these pages right now and, as a result of that "chance" encounter, become a Christian. Don't you think that would be wonderful? No, do more than that: pray for it to happen—because there is no such thing as "chance"!

RESPOND

WEDNESDAY

THE DAUGHTERS OF JERUSALEM

Luke 23:27-31

Jesus will engage in more conversation before he breathes his last; but these words constitute his final public address.

A large crowd follows the dismal procession as it makes its way to the crucifixion site at the place called The Skull. Some have come to mock Jesus; but there are others who have come to support him. The latter are "mourning and lamenting for him" (v 27). It is a pitiful scene.

Few, if any, readers of these pages will have witnessed an execution, and fewer still a public execution. In Jesus' day, women would attend crucifixions in order to minister to the condemned person during their slow agony, perhaps taking with them wine mixed with gall that might help deaden the terrible pain (as in Matthew 27:34—the wine which Jesus refused). A group of such women wept loudly as they accompanied Jesus on his way to the cross. He now turns to address them. We might expect Jesus to say a word of gratitude. But instead he speaks a word of loving warning. Why?

For one thing, he does not need their tears, nor can their lamentations comfort him—for he is going to a comfortless place. More than that, he knows that his crisis will soon be over, and that his suffering, while extreme, has a glorious purpose—our salvation. But for these Jerusalem women and their children, the future holds days of such horror that barrenness will be seen as a blessing, not a curse (as it was normally regarded). The coming crisis will be so great that people will cry out to the mountains to fall on them and the hills to cover them in a bid to end it. For if crucifixion happens to Jesus "when the wood is green", then "what will happen when it is dry?" (23:31). Perhaps this was a proverbial saying. Perhaps in this context it means, *If this is what happens to the innocent Saviour, what will befall those who reject him?* Surely some great tragedy awaits them. "Weep for yourselves," says Jesus (v 28).

As Jesus had prophesied (21:20-24), in AD 70 the city of Jerusalem was besieged by the Roman army and destroyed along with the temple. But what he had anticipated happening to the citizens of Jerusalem then, while real and terrible, was but a precursor of the great final day of the judgment of God:

> *When he opened the sixth seal, I looked, and behold, there was a great earthquake, and the sun became black as sackcloth, the full moon became like blood, and the stars of the sky fell to the earth as the fig tree sheds its winter fruit when shaken by a gale. The sky vanished ... and every mountain and island was removed from its place. Then the kings of the earth and the great ones and the generals and the rich and the powerful, and everyone, slave and free, hid themselves in the caves and among the rocks of the mountains, calling to the mountains and rocks, "Fall on us and hide us from the face of him who is seated on the throne, and from the wrath of the Lamb, for*

the great day of their wrath has come, and who can stand?" (Revelation 6:12-17)

If the judgment that is to be poured out on sin is "the wrath of the Lamb", who came to save sinners—how tragic not to weep for ourselves; and how foolish not to be driven by our tears to find a hiding place in Christ. For even if the mountains could fall on us, the caves and the rocks could not hide us from the face of him who is seated on the throne. One glance will tell us all we need to know: outside of Christ, we stand condemned.

The women of Jerusalem needed to know that if all they saw was that Jesus needed their sympathy, then they had misunderstood him altogether. He was carrying the judgment of God against the sin of the world. Unless they found a hiding place in him, no amount of sympathy would save them from the events of the future. And the same is true of us.

REFLECT

- There is a huge difference between a sentimental view of the cross—which stirs up a self-gratifying feeling of sadness—and a serious view of it—which focuses soberly on Christ. Which view are you closer to? Run now to Jesus as he is: your hiding place.

RESPOND

THURSDAY

THE TWO CRIMINALS

Luke 23:32, 39-43

The Gospels have sometimes been described as passion narratives with extended introductions. There is an element of truth in this. Luke spends two chapters on the first twelve years of Jesus' life, sixteen chapters on the final three years, and then six chapters on the final week. It is with a view to this week that Jesus lived all previous weeks. So the action is slowed down, frame by frame as it were, to help us to meditate on and take in the significance of what is happening—for clearly this part of the Gospel is the key to the whole.

Now Luke devotes two whole chapters to the closing twenty-four hours of Jesus' life. It is with a view to these hours that Jesus has lived all his previous hours.

And here, slowing down even further, Luke devotes five verses to a conversation that may have lasted only a minute or two. But in one sense, it is with a view to what Jesus would accomplish in these few minutes that he lived all previous minutes.

The man who was my minister in my mid-teens once told me, "I've discovered that most people die the way they lived". He was by no means a man to doubt "death-bed con-versions". It was simply that he had seen very few of them. His words were certainly true of one of the men crucified beside Jesus. Crucifixion was a cruel punishment—a linger-ing death by slow asphyxiation that often took days to ac-complish. The man was in pain, utterly helpless, with every moment making him long that it would end. Whatever anger had led to the crime for which he was being punished, he was angry still and directed his violent emotions towards Jesus: *If you are the Christ, why don't you save us?*

Perhaps it is understandable. We know that the law never works grace: punishment does not make us love; in and of itself it may produce regret, but it cannot produce repent-ance. Only the hope of forgiveness can produce repentance. But there was no hope of forgiveness here, nor any desire for it: no sorrow; no repentance. Only more anger.

But from the opposite side came a voice struggling for breath to speak a few words in Jesus' defence. Something had happened in this man's heart. The exchange that fol-lowed has many facets.

- He confessed his guilt: "We are receiving the due re-ward for our deeds" (v 41).
- He recognised Jesus' innocence: "This man has done nothing wrong" (v 41).
- He sought mercy: "Jesus, remember me" (v 42).
- He confessed Jesus' lordship: " ... when you come into your kingdom" (v 42).
- He was given gospel hope: "Today you will be with me in paradise" (v 43).

In these last moments of lucidity, this dear man gives ev-idence that his heart has been transformed. He becomes the first witness for the defence of the crucified Christ, rebuking the other criminal and saying, "Do you not fear God?" (v 40).

We're reminded of this moment in the words of William Cowper's hymn "There is a fountain filled with blood":

> *The dying thief rejoiced to see*
> *That fountain in his day.*

And we can marvel that, by faith, that same thief could, with us, go on to sing…

> *When this poor, lisping, stammering tongue*
> *Lies silent in the grave,*
> *Then in a nobler, sweeter song,*
> *I'll sing your power to save.*

REFLECT

- Turn the bullet points above into your own prayer to the Lord Jesus; enjoy his words of reassurance in verse 43; and respond with a hymn of praise.

RESPOND

GOOD FRIDAY

THE FATHER

Luke 23:44-49

Jesus' third "word" from the cross recorded by Luke is "Father, into your hands I commit my spirit" (v 46), following which he "breathed his last". For Luke, this is not only Jesus' final word from the cross; it is also the last clue he gives us to the inner significance of what is happening at The Skull.

On the road to Jerusalem we have eavesdropped on many of Jesus' encounters with others. But only one of them parallels this moment. Here we have the consummation of what took place in Gethsemane. Here—as there—it is his own Father whom Jesus "encounters". While he refers to him frequently in this Gospel, there are only three places where he addresses him directly (10:21-22; 22:42 and 23:46).

In Gethsemane our Lord's human will had struggled to submit to the will of his Father—for his holy soul necessarily shrank from the implications of drinking the cup the Father was giving him. There he was being asked to be willing to do what he could not desire to do—namely, to drink the cup of the wrath of God and experience the terrible sense of abandonment that would result. But here

TO SEEK AND TO SAVE

the same holy Saviour is confidently committing his spirit into his Father's care.

What has happened? What has changed between the desperate plea in Gethsemane and this confident declaration at The Skull? Luke gives us two clues:

Clue 1: In the Roman Empire the day began at 6:00 a.m. It was now "about the sixth hour": noon—the time of day when the sun was ordinarily at is zenith. But not that day. For the next three hours the land was shrouded in darkness. Luke records this as a *fact*, but there can be no doubt that he also sees it as a *sign*—an event with deep significance. The heavens became opaque and impenetrable. For a brief season, creation itself seemed to be thrown into reverse gear and God said, *Let there NOT be light* (in contrast to Genesis 1:3). His face no longer shone on the earth. More to the point, the Aaronic benediction ("The LORD bless you and keep you; *the LORD make his face to shine upon you* ... the LORD *lift up his countenance upon you* and give you peace", Numbers 6:24-26) had ceased to function. Jesus' experience was the reverse of that of David, who was able to say, "Even though I walk through the valley of the shadow of death ... you are with me" (Psalm 23:4). Nature itself put on the dark clothes of mourning as Christ the Creator was put to death by sinful men, and on the cross came under the curse of God (Galatians 3:13).

Clue 2: Luke records another event. The massive curtain of the temple was torn in two (23:45). Rending a garment was a sign of grief, of death and of mourning. Was God rending his "temple garments" at the death of his beloved Son? Perhaps. But more than that, he was de-consecrating the Jerusalem temple. The temple curtain was now no longer the barrier between God and man. Not only the temple veil but the flesh of Christ had been torn to create the new and living way into his presence (Hebrews 10:20).

Jesus' work was completed; so now, he called out "with a loud voice" of triumph and joy, "Father, into your hands I commit my spirit!" (23:46). Was he still meditating on the Psalms? If so, he was now well past Psalm 22:1 ("My God, my God, why have you forsaken me?") and had reached Psalm 31:5 ("Into your hand I commit my spirit"). But more than that, he was now calling God "Father" again. Luke adds simply, "And having said this he breathed his last".

Jesus' obedience to his Father, and his suffering, had a passive dimension; he was crucified by the hands of wicked and cruel men. But he had also been actively obedient: "obedient to the point of death, even death on a cross" (Philippians 2:8).

His work was finished now. It was time to go home to the Father. He breathed a sigh of relief and committed himself into his hands.

At the foot of the cross, the soldiers in his execution squad did not notice that Jesus had died (John 19:33)—they had been too interested in casting lots to see who would win his clothes, and joining in the general abuse of him, to care about what he said. But not so the centurion who commanded them. He observed what had happened and said, "Certainly this man was innocent!" And his response? "He praised God" (v 47).

So should we.

REFLECT

- There are many reasons to love the Lord Jesus. Today express your love for him because for your sake he lived his entire life, moment by moment, in loving obedience to his heavenly Father—not least when it was most difficult.

RESPOND

SATURDAY

THE GOOD MAN

Luke 23:50-56

Luke wants you to admire Joseph of Arimathea. He was "a good and righteous man" (v 50). That meant he was faithful to God's covenant and experienced its blessings. Like some others in this Gospel, he was "looking"— waiting expectantly—for God's kingdom to come. He was also a member of the Sanhedrin but had not consented to its condemnation of Jesus (perhaps its leaders had avoided summoning to the crisis meeting anyone whose loyalties they suspected). Matthew and John tell us explicitly what Luke only implies: he was also a rich man (he already owned a tomb in Jerusalem); and he was a secret disciple who, until this point, had lacked the courage to confess it (Matthew 27:57; John 19:38).

The Sanhedrin was a very select group of well-connected men. Word of mouth travelled fast in Jerusalem. Joseph must soon have learned what had happened. Jesus was dead.

It was now or never for Joseph. He stepped out of the shadows, went directly to Pilate and asked for the body. This was not without risk, or cost. *If* Pilate granted his request, and Joseph personally handled Jesus' body, he would be rendering himself ritually unclean. But he knew that otherwise Jesus' body would probably be thrown into a common grave where the bones of many criminals already lay—perhaps right there at The Skull (was this the derivation of the name?). Some things are far more important than ritual purity.

Pilate was probably relieved. Now he could relax and forget about the problem of Jesus. Little did he know... But for Joseph there must have been three hours of feverish activity. It was already past three o'clock and the Jewish Sabbath began at six o' clock—not a lot of time to get to Pilate for permission, get back to The Skull, arrange helpers, and carry Jesus' body to the family tomb.

Why does Luke pay so much attention to Jesus' burial? For several reasons. The first is that he removes any doubt about the reality of Jesus' death. The Roman soldiers had made sure of that. Joseph had himself handled the body, and others had helped him prepare it for burial and carry it to the tomb. The second is that Luke makes clear that there was no confusion about the location of Jesus' burial place. Joseph's tomb was new, and a variety of witnesses knew where it was.

Then, thirdly, Luke adds that the women went to prepare spices and ointments to return after the Sabbath to anoint the body. In other words, nobody—despite what Jesus had taught them—was expecting Jesus' resurrection.

But before we come to that resurrection, we should take another look at Joseph. Of all the Gospel-writers, Luke was most like a historian in his method. But historians can also be poets and theologians. And there is something poetically theological about the way he frames his whole Gospel. His story of Jesus' life begins with him being cared for by a man named Joseph, who places him in a borrowed resting place, in which no baby had ever been laid. It ends with Jesus being cared for again by a man named Joseph, who lays him in another borrowed resting place, where no man had ever been laid. The story has come full circle; another Joseph has received Christ into his heart and life. At the turning point of Luke's Gospel, near the beginning of the journey to Jerusalem, Jesus had said that discipleship meant following one who had "nowhere to lay his head" (9:58). Now Joseph had come out into the open as a disciple, whatever it might cost. So he gave up to Jesus the place where he had planned to lay his own head.

At the cross, Jesus had given up what was his for the sake of Joseph. Now Joseph was giving up what was his for the sake of Jesus. That is what it means to be a disciple.

REFLECT

- The gospel is sometimes called "the great exchange". Christ took our place and gave himself for us. But that leads to another exchange: we give ourselves to Christ and live for him. Is there a way in which the Spirit is prompting you to recommit yourself to this second exchange?

RESPOND

EASTER SUNDAY

THE TWO EN ROUTE HOME

Luke 24:13-35, 50-52

In Shakespeare's play *Hamlet*, the young Prince of Denmark ponders how to expose the guilt of his step-father, Claudius, who, he believes, has murdered his father. A troop of itinerant actors appears. Hamlet arranges for them to perform a play with a plot that echoes the facts of his father's death: "The play's the thing wherein I'll catch the conscience of the king". This "play within the play" reveals the truth.

Luke employs a similar technique—he tells the story of a journey within a journey. This shorter journey explains the meaning of the longer journey that has occupied most of the Gospel (from Luke 9:51 onwards). Now everything becomes clear.

It is the first Easter Sunday. Two disciples are on their way to Emmaus. One is named Cleopas (v 18); the other, unnamed, is perhaps his wife. (They seem to return to their own home in v 29.) They are dejected in the aftermath of Jesus' crucifixion; they are also confused by reports of an empty tomb and by rumours of angels saying that Jesus is alive.

A stranger catches up with them on the way and asks them what they have been discussing. How can he not be familiar with the one topic on everybody's lips? They are amazed at the stranger's ignorance of the fact that Jesus is dead. Nevertheless—not realising they are in for a shock!— they explain the events that have dashed their hopes. *Oh,* says the stranger, *You are so foolish and slow!* And patiently he takes them on a brief journey through a whole series of passages in the Old Testament. He shows them how what has happened is exactly what Scripture promised would happen to the Messiah!

They are almost home now. But the stranger's company has warmed this pair's hearts. They don't want him to leave. And so he stays for a meal. Perhaps conscious that they are in the presence of someone much greater than themselves, they either ask him, or wait for him, to say the traditional blessing. But as he takes the bread, blesses it and breaks it, a light goes on in their minds. He reminds them of someone! And perhaps they also see the marks on his hands and wrists as he breaks the bread.

It is Jesus!

And then, just as suddenly as he appeared, he was gone!

The two look at each other: *Did you feel what I felt while we were talking on the road? Was your heart burning too?* They rush back to Jerusalem and burst into the upper room to tell the others that Jesus is alive; he has risen from the dead! Do they have a moment of deflation when they discover that the other disciples already know? But nobody seems to care who found out first. The only thing that matters is that Jesus has risen and is alive—just as he promised.

The journey to Jerusalem began with the disciples noticing a look on Jesus' face that they could not understand. En route they watched him encountering and transforming many lives. By the time they were making their way to Emmaus, they were consumed with grief and, doubtless, with deep personal regret that they had failed him so badly. But the journey had not finished. Now, at last, they understand.

Jerusalem was the destination for Jesus, but it was not the end of the journey for his disciples. Now they knew that just as he had set his face to go to Jerusalem, they must set their faces to go to all nations to proclaim his gospel and to call people to repentance and faith in him (24:45-47).

The journey of Christ to Jerusalem led to the journey of his gospel to the nations, and to us. Now we are on a journey to bring that same gospel to others.

But if you are to join that journey, you need to share the experience of Cleopas and his companion. You need to have Jesus open your mind to understand the Scriptures. You need to have Jesus move your heart so that it burns with the thrill of realising that you have a crucified Saviour who has risen from the dead and who is with you. Because you surely do, and he surely has, and he surely is.

REFLECT
- Today we reach the end of the journey to Jerusalem. Are you ready to continue the journey *from* Jerusalem, as you take the gospel to others? What might that look like over the next few days, weeks, months and years?

RESPOND

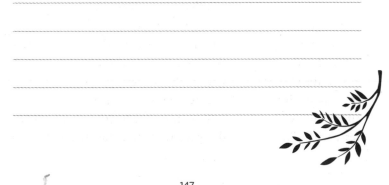

EXTRA SPACE TO RESPOND

COMPANY

BIBLICAL | RELEVANT | ACCESSIBLE

At The Good Book Company, we are dedicated to helping Christians and local churches grow. We believe that God's growth process always starts with hearing clearly what he has said to us through his timeless word—the Bible.

Ever since we opened our doors in 1991, we have been striving to produce Bible-based resources that bring glory to God. We have grown to become an international provider of user-friendly resources to the Christian community, with believers of all backgrounds and denominations using our books, Bible studies, devotionals, evangelistic resources, and DVD-based courses.

We want to equip ordinary Christians to live for Christ day by day, and churches to grow in their knowledge of God, their love for one another, and the effectiveness of their outreach.

Call us for a discussion of your needs or visit one of our local websites for more information on the resources and services we provide.

Your friends at The Good Book Company

thegoodbook.com | thegoodbook.co.uk
thegoodbook.com.au | thegoodbook.co.nz
thegoodbook.co.in